Old Words Open New Worlds

S.B. Keshava Swami

S.B. Keshava Swami

Contact the publisher via team@keshavaswami.com

First print: July 2023, 3000 copies

ISBN: 978-1-7394681-0-1

Editing & Proofing: Bhaja Govindam Das, Prerna Agarwal, Dev Manani, Pratik Agarwal

Front Cover: Sofie Alsbo

Layout & Design: Yogendra Sahu

Photography:
© Ananta Vrindavan
© ISKCON Bhaktivedanta Manor (Various photographers)

The International Society for Krishna Consciousness
Founder Acarya: His Divine Grace A.C. Bhaktivedanta Swami Prabhupada

www.keshavaswami.com
www.schoolofbhakti.com
www.thinkgita.org

Dedicated to those who have the curiosity and courage
to challenge everything the world told them to be.

Fortune favours the bold.

CONTENTS

PROGRESSIVE DISRUPTION

The world will never be the same again. Everything from entertainment, to education, to eating, evolves at an exponential rate. The disruptive brands of our time - Apple, Amazon, Uber, Netflix and the like - appeared from nowhere and have ended up everywhere. They dared to be different, challenged the status quo and displaced the modus operandi. Their innovations have changed the way we function.

Disruption, however, is not the monopoly of the tech savvy giants. Since the beginning of time, spiritual disruptors have periodically entered the stage, challenged the world and changed the game. Material disruptors intently ask whether there's a *better way to do things*. The spiritual disruptors table a heavier interrogation - they question whether there are *better things we could be doing*. Material disruptors challenge the *how* and the *what*, while spiritual disruptors challenge the *why*. Material disruptors change *products and processes*. Spiritual disruptors change *philosophy* - the very foundation of truth and the core of what we accept to be real and valuable.

I am a self-confessed victim of the spiritual disruptors. When they started dropping bombs of wisdom before me, it shook my world. Aspirations and plans that I previously held in high esteem were being obliterated and the landscape of my life was dramatically reconstructed before my eyes. I was becoming more aware, more conscious and more

8

Contents

purposeful. I realised that till that point, my entire worldview had been founded upon blind acceptance of so-called truths. Those disruptors were messengers of 'old words' – 'old words' which were opening up 'new worlds.' Going against the grain wasn't easy, but the excitement, adventure and intrigue was generating a hunger to keep on exploring. Looking back, I marvel at how that disruption helped me progress to a beautiful new paradigm.

The Vedas are the oldest body of spiritual literature known to humankind. There, tucked away in mystical Sanskrit *sutras*, are profound insights into the self, the universe and the deeper purpose behind existence. Those 'old words' are known as *tattva* – essential truths and principles which underpin universal reality. *Tattva* stands true in all times, all places and all circumstances, transcending sectarian belief. Deep comprehension of those truths empowers one to unravel any existential mystery and upgrade themselves on every conceivable level – physically, emotionally, socially and most importantly, spiritually.

For over two decades I've tried to study these ancient books, particularly the Bhagavad-gita, utilising that *tattva* to decode the events, experiences and emotions of life. As a monk, presenting that *tattva* to audiences through the written and spoken word became my day job (unpaid ofcourse!). In that humble endeavour, a deep conviction grew within me – *this is wisdom that breathes*! It's living, it's real and it perfectly relates to the human condition.

In the first part of this book, I share writings and reflections from the last five years of my life (2018-2022), which have been the most eventful, challenging and transformative so far. Over this period, the world was turned upside down as we contended with a global pandemic. I also witnessed some of my closest confidants depart from the world. On a personal level, I passed through a major juncture in my own spiritual journey when I embraced vows of lifetime renunciation. Through all these chapters, the pen (and keyboard) became my constant go-to. While scribing my thoughts I'd express, clarify, process and comprehend many things. While editing my words, it felt as though I was editing my consciousness. Most importantly, seeing life through the lens of *tattva* brought an elevated perspective, where life and it's lessons became strikingly apparent to me.

The second part of Tattva details my responses to interesting questions I've been asked over the years. The inquiries span everything from philosophy to food and leadership to love, asked by the curious, the challenging and also the committed. We hope it will give a taste of how versatile this *tattva* is in addressing the needs, interests and concerns that resound within each and every one of us.

I conclude this book by offering some words of gratitude to my spiritual teachers who progressively disrupted my life. The post-modern mind often rebels against authority figures and the principle of gurus. I try, however, to show how these beautiful relationships have been powerful and integral to my spiritual evolution. My firm conviction is that nobody is self-made.

BHAGAVAD GĪTĀ AS IT IS

HIS DIVINE GRACE
A. C. BHAKTIVEDANTA SWAMI PRABHUPĀDA
Founder-*Ācārya* of the International Society for Krishna Consciousness

The most widely distributed translation of the Bhagavad-gita in the world

THE JEWEL BOX

The Vedas are vast. They amount to hundreds of thousands of verses, dealing with the topics of this world and beyond. The broadness and depth of the Vedas make for its beauty, but also its difficulty. Finding the essence is not an easy task. Thus, certain books within the Vedic corpus are highlighted as principle – they powerfully bring forth the most essential wisdom that everyone needs to grasp. In one famed verse, the entire collection of the Vedas is compared to a cow and Krishna is said to be the milker of that cow. The milk, that miracle food which nourishes the future generations, is the beautiful Bhagavad-gita. Many have concurred – if we had to choose a single book which encapsulates the most powerful and pertinent philosophical truths of the East, we would certainly choose the Bhagavad-gita.

In the 700-verse conversation between Krishna and Arjuna, the most fundamental questions, deepest aspirations, recurring obstacles and essential conclusions are discussed. It is considered the most comprehensive treatise on yoga, or spiritual connection – the desire that sits deep within every single living being. The scholar-saint, Visvanatha Cakravarti Thakur, further compares the Bhagavad-gita to a Jewel Box. The base and the lid, he says, constitute the two 'outer layers' of the yoga system – *karma-yoga* and *jnana-yoga*. The middle, where the jewel majestically rests, is considered the quintessence of yoga – *bhakti-yoga*.

650 year old handwritten manuscripts of Bhagavad-gita & Srimad Bhagavatam

In modern terminology, we could say the three systems of yoga encompass how to live (*karma-yoga*), how to love (*bhakti-yoga*) and how to let go (*jnana-yoga*).

While the ultimate treasure is carefully nestled in the middle, the outer teachings of *karma-yoga* and *jnana-yoga* are not inconsequential. We exist in the complexity of modern civilisation and learning to function here in a spiritual way, remaining unaffected and unattached, is a hard task. The Bhagavad-gita offers unique insights, and thus, along with ultimate aspirations, it also addresses immediate pressures. The Gita deals with the life of here along with the life of after. It is the ultimate in self-development – helping us to rediscover authenticity, redefine success, revive our purpose, reposition our lifestyle, reconfigure our energies and, most importantly, re-encounter Divinity and re-awaken pure love. In short, Krishna empowers us to rethink life.

He bases the presentation around five essential *tattvas*, which are clear, concise, logical and scientific – not just appealing to faith, belief, personality, or culture. In all the articles, writings and responses to questions, we invariably touch on one or more of these *tattvas*, which are as follows:

Tattva 1: Soul (*atma*) - Our physical body is nothing more than a costume. We are spirit souls; the consciousness which animates the body. This life is merely one chapter in a much longer story.

Tattva 2: Material World (*prakrti*) - The world is a cosmic university, wired to awaken wisdom. Though we come here to enjoy life through material pursuits, we invariably end up questioning – *"Is there a deeper meaning to life?"*

Tattva 3: Activities (*karma*) - The law of action and reaction is nature's way to educate and evolve us. Good actions are materially rewarded, bad actions are punished, while spiritual actions free us from karmic entanglement and awaken spiritual happiness.

Tattva 4: Time (*kala*) - Our life, the universe and everything in material existence moves according to the wheel of time. Time strips us of everything - an uncomfortable reality. We naturally seek eternity since our real self is spiritual.

Tattva 5: God (*isvara*) - Our 'human journey' is an opportunity to reawaken our eternal relationship with God and return to the spiritual world, where every step is a dance and every word a song. Krishna explains how to do this through yoga, which literally means 'to link.'

In essence: God sets the world in motion, mediating it through the mechanism of time. The soul's journey in this world is governed by the law of karma. Yoga allows the soul to reconnect with the eternal reality and exit this unnatural situation.

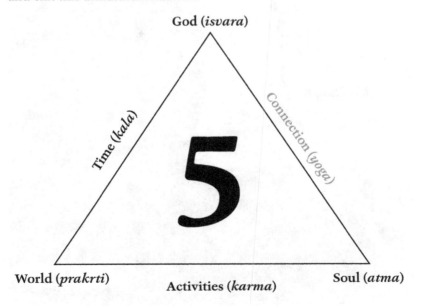

God (*isvara*)

Time (*kala*)

Connection (*yoga*)

World (*prakrti*)

Activities (*karma*)

Soul (*atma*)

Srila Prabhupada in New York (1965)

SWAMI ON SKID ROW

Since the beginning of time, the saintly teachers have carried the 'old words' of scripture into the modern climate. They were not just teachers and orators, but living examples of the Bhagavad-gita who could bring the wisdom alive and instigate revolutionary transformations.

A.C. Bhaktivedanta Swami Prabhupada was one of those illustrious, saintly teachers - a spiritual disruptor of the highest calibre. In 1966, at the age of 69, homeless, penniless and alone, he arrived in the Lower East Side of New York, searching for 'better opportunities' to share the message of the Gita. This was Skid row; the lowest of the low. Here he lived, worshiped, studied and taught. Every evening, his decrepit residence, the rat-ridden 94 Bowery, would fill up with buzzing acidheads, bearded bohemians, ruined alcoholics and disillusioned dropouts. Sex, music, LSD and consciousness expansion; that's what made them tick. The Swami would nonchalantly step into the makeshift 'temple' and take his seat at the front, face-to-face with these confused souls who were looking for real love, real happiness and real spiritual experience.

The Swami was unfazed; his expression exuding bottomless depth and boundless compassion. In short, straight-forward philosophical discourses, he delivered eternal truths with resounding impact. When he sang in simple tunes with a bongo drum, their heads would spin and their hearts were conquered. His tremendous devotion empowered his urgent message to penetrate the depths of their consciousness. He effortlessly smashed layers of illusion, unrelentingly exposing the fallacy of all materialistic ideology.

From these humble beginnings, Prabhupada went on to establish the International Society for Krishna Consciousness (ISKCON) and in a few short years made 'Hare Krishna' a household name. He circled the globe fourteen times, opened over a hundred temples, launched a variety of spiritual welfare projects, authored volumes of books, and made genuine spirituality inspiring, practical and accessible for people from all walks of life. No amount of social commentary, historical analysis or anthropological conjecture can account for his incredible achievements. Prabhupada's story is tangible proof of a spiritual miracle that defied all odds. His life and teachings remain the strength, inspiration and guiding light for millions and counting.

My writings and reflections are primarily based on Srila Prabhupada's Bhagavad-Gita As It Is, the world's most popular and widely read edition of the ancient classic. It has been translated in over sixty languages and is available in nearly every major city in the world. I've never encountered anyone who has communicated spiritual truth with such conviction, clarity, creativity and compassion. His words are harder than a thunderbolt yet softer than a rose.

Srila Prabhupada was deeply concerned that ancient truths be carried into the modern context in suitable language and with reference to the contemporary needs, interests and concerns of the people. His predecessor, Srila Bhaktivinoda Thakura, another prolific writer, explained how many people simply study books, collect information and then store those facts, like a magistrate imprisons a criminal in jail. He labelled it *"fruitless retention."* Rather, he said, one should take such knowledge, sincerely apply it in one's life and then creatively share it according to personal experience and taste.

I can only pray that my imperfect words will do some justice to the 'old words' of the scriptures and the saints, to successfully open 'new worlds' for my esteemed readers.

S.B. Keshava Swami

Writing can be seen as an exercise in self-development. It's an opportunity to crystallize thoughts and test comprehension since explaining a subject matter necessitates that one have a good understanding of it first. While communicating universal spiritual truths, our own weaknesses, faults and deficiencies become strikingly apparent. Scribing our thoughts can reveal the mysteries within. It also helps one to become more conscious of the world around them. Everyday occurrences and interactions are pregnant with insightful life lessons. Being in writing mode helps one to tune in. We may read wisdom in a book, but we see it in action in the real world.

John Howard Griffin, a biographer of Catholic monk, Thomas Merton, writes: "His most vital writing is private, what he did for himself, because he made constant notes to help clarify things for himself. He thought and sought to express experience on paper as a self-guide rather than to reveal anything. He sought to get rid of the role, to flee the "role" of the monk in order to become the monk. To be and not merely to appear to be. These are great and profound differences which few perceive, even in the religious life."

THINK OUT
LOUD
Writings & Reflections

OBSERVING LIFE

As people get older, the past tends to dominate their consciousness. Sitting in a rocking chair and reminiscing seems natural since the majority of life is behind them. Young people, on the other hand, tend to restlessly project into the future – desires and dreams of what's to come dominates their attention. In middle age, however, we're best placed to do both – look back on our experiences, draw the lessons and then factor them into our future planning. We get the best of both worlds, since we can reflect like the old and also plan like the young. Ironically, most people do neither!

Wisdom doesn't simply come from experience; it comes from deeply contemplating those experiences and then remodelling our approach to life. I've always found writing to be a powerful means to do this. It has helped me to be more conscious and reflective about the past, present and future. I started blogging in 2008 and it became one of my most important self-development tools. In this section, I share some of my thoughts and reflections as I observe life and everything that happens around us.

NAKED TRUTH (SEP 2017)

On 2nd September, the BBC reported that a public park near the French capital Paris has designated an area for nudists. The site, as large as a football pitch, will be open until 15th October as part of a temporary experiment. There are measures to avoid misuse, but the overall idea is to have an *"open-minded vision for the use of Parisian parks."* Naturists predict that thousands will flock to the park, while the more conservative contingent are deeming the whole initiative *"crazy."* Paris already has one public pool where people can swim naked three times a week.

Does nudity and naturality go hand-in-hand? What could be the possible repercussions? Is nakedness a progressive way forward?

I guess the more noble proponents of nudity are searching for more authenticity, more purity, more freedom, more naturalness and more equality. In a world riddled with superficiality and 'cover-ups' you can appreciate the attempt to strip away the external layers. Maybe that will facilitate more genuine interactions, relationships and community. Maybe we need to break down artificial taboos and find our true self. All good sentiments, no doubt. But is nudity really the way forward?

Yoga wisdom begins with a foundational understanding of identity. The physical body and the subtle mind, sages explain, are simply coverings of the soul. In 1965, Swami Prabhupada, freshly arrived from India, visited a hippie commune to share his spiritual insights. He took to the stage and with eyes closed, began meditatively singing. When he gazed out some minutes later he saw a huge crowd... most of whom were completely naked! Addressing this phenomenon, the Swami quipped: *"I can see you like to take your clothes off – so now we invite you to go beyond the conception of the body, which itself is an artificial covering of the soul!"*

In the attempt to shed some layers, nudity can drape us into a thicker illusion. If we are not our bodies, then unrestricted exposure may well cause us to become more entrenched in that misconception. By covering up, we create the necessary sobriety to find our deeper identity. We need to redirect the focus from the physical to the spiritual. Stripping down may well increase the superficiality. Rather than campaigning for naked bodies, let's search for the naked truth. Then we'll find true freedom, equality, authenticity and naturalness.

PROUD BLOCK (FEB 2018)

Pride is a formidable block on the road of spirituality. When it rears its ugly head it's embarrassingly obvious – to ourselves and others. We may deny it, cover it up or justify it, but deep down we know something is out of tune. A mentor once told me that there is a fine net covering the spiritual reality and only those who become small enough to fit through the holes can access it. Hard as they try, the big-headed inevitably get stuck. There is no room for pride in the life of a progressive spiritualist.

A proud person can't LAST. Pride generates destructive thoughts, words and actions, erecting huge barriers in our relationships. It's a corrosive disease which makes people insensitive, arrogant and practically impossible to joyfully get along with. Pride prevents us from deeply connecting with spiritual company, without which there is no question of spiritual progression. If we can't appreciate the people around us, we'll lose them. Time and time again we observe how proud people, sooner or later, lose their enthusiasm to continue.

And even if they do continue, consider:

A proud person can't LEARN. In colloquial English we say a proud person is *"full of it."* It's a graphic term – there is no space to introduce anything new. Pride and the stubbornness which accompanies it, blocks us from discovering, improving, transforming and evolving. Not only does pride create artificiality, but it maintains it and breeds it. Proud people never really develop any substance. After years and years of spiritual practice, they find they haven't actually learnt that much.

And even if they do learn many things, consider:

A proud person can't LOVE. Pride transforms us into little gods ruling over our imaginary kingdoms. The thought of being a servant becomes more and more alien, creating a disposition fuelled by expectation and demands. It is the spirit of selflessness, however, which is the foundation upon which deep loving relationships are built. While we are unable to genuinely place ourselves in the humble position, we'll find our connections with man and God remain superficial, transactional and unsatisfying.

Praying for genuine humility, we remind ourselves – if we are proud, we can't last, we can't learn and ultimately, we can't love.

"A proud man is always looking down on things and people; and, of course, as long as you are looking down, you cannot see something that is above you." (C.S. Lewis)

INDUCED SELFLESSNESS (FEB 2018)

Should I get married or become a monk? Which one is best?

It's a question people ask me time and time again. It's also a question which can't be answered off-the-cuff. Imagine going into a hospital and inquiring which operation is the best. It's illogical. Unless they sign you in, observe your symptoms, run some tests and peruse the results, they can't really offer any substantial guidance. Everyone is different and everyone therefore requires something different. Thus, in the traditions of yore, people would take the first twenty years of their life to 'run some tests' and understand their psycho-physical temperament. After all, it's difficult to hear the heart in the noise of life – busyness, expectation, social hype and the hard struggle for existence blocks us from finding ourselves. Taking 'time out' to prepare oneself for a lifetime of solid spirituality is absolutely essential. We can't jump the gun.

Whilst contemplating the two life paths, however, something did occur to me. Last week I was with a good friend while his energetic four-year-old son bustled about. Now that young boy was demanding! Having never experienced that kind of responsibility, I was fascinated to observe their interactions. The care, attention, empathy and incredible patience that went into the interaction prompted a striking epiphany. Family commitments, as father and mother especially, undoubtedly usher one into a heightened state of selflessness. It's so strikingly induced upon you that you can't avoid it. You quickly accept that life is not just about what you want – you're forced to put others before you. If one can deeply internalise such lessons, they can serve as crucial realisations on the spiritual journey. When it comes to qualities like selflessness, parents have more than just book knowledge. In that sense, family life does have a unique advantage.

Life as a solo renunciant doesn't offer the same inducement. It's easier to sit back and conveniently select when to extend and when to retreat. One has more scope to withdraw from the social demands as and when they please. While it may seem advantageous and supportive of one's spirituality, it can also stunt one's progress. Renunciates are not forced to develop selflessness in the same way. It's not that they can't, since we see distinguished renunciates who do go above and beyond the call of duty. But they have to make the extra special *voluntary* push to help and serve others, lest that sense of selflessness never really arises. From the externals, renunciates are giving their all. Speaking for myself, however, I regularly pull back and find some space whenever I like. If my general tendency is towards comfort and doing less than necessary, it's dangerous. How ironic if I would live a lifetime of renunciation and still remain self-centred. It's something I often reflect upon.

THE VISION OF ETERNITY (MAR 2021)

My eyes opened at 2.00am today. Unable to sleep, I showered and went down to the Patrons office. When I walked in I saw the smiling portrait of Srutidharma Das. On this day, one year ago, he left the world. He invested the entirety of his being into serving everyone and everything around him. Everywhere we look, in projects, people and places, we feel his influence – physically departed, but present as ever. As with many others, he smiled on me. He told me to write, to speak, to take risks, to become humble, tolerant and give one life in selfless service... he gave me a vision for my life.

At 7.30am I sat down in the temple room for the daily wisdom discussion. The verse for the day read: *"The value of a moment's association with a devotee of the Lord cannot be compared even with the value of attaining the heavenly planets or liberation from matter and what to speak of worldly benedictions in the form of material prosperity, which are for those who are meant for death."* What magic! It's one of the extremely rare verses of the Srimad-Bhagavatam that appear twice, verbatim (1.18.3 & 4.30.34). Not just chance, more likely a confirmation from Krishna. When extraordinary fortune arises, the saints appear in our life.

Though small in stature, Srutidharma Das was a spiritual giant. He built communities, mentored hundreds of individuals, delivered inspired spiritual teachings and, in the process, sacrificed all comfort without a second thought. He held back nothing and it was my great fortune to witness this on a day-to-day basis for over two decades. He never changed – his dedication, devotion and unbreakable determination were entrenched within his entire being.

Srutidharma lived with the vision of eternity. Though he never verbalised his full realisation to me, I observed how he exuded an aloofness from the world, realising he was here on a sole mission of selfless service. Everything separate from that was a waste of time. Srutidharma hardly slept and ate even less. Always on the go, meeting the needs of the day and rising to any challenge. He was adored by so many, but never stopped to bask in that glory, convinced that aspirations for name, fame and prestige were useless disturbances... ethereal allurements.

Srutidharma accepted a heavyweight level of responsibility which invariably invited complexity, anxiety, criticism and negativity. Even the saintly are not spared. He navigated that thorny path with grace and resilience, never becoming frustrated or fatigued. There was no question of throwing in the towel. He turned up every single day on top form. *"Get up, dress up, show up"* he told me, *"this is the most important work in the world."* He knew his business and he kept going on and on and on.

The story doesn't end there. Though Srutidharma's impressive list of personal achievements is endless, he was interested in something more. Devoid of envy, he loved to see the success of others. He wanted to see everyone at their best and spent his days encouraging, empowering, appreciating and convincing people to believe in themselves. He

Srutidharma Das (1958 - 2020)

wasn't just great, but he made others great. Not just that, but he trained those people to help others in the same way. Who can fathom how far his legacy will reach?

Srutidharma Das – a powerful, illustrious, global leader – was also someone you could just hang out with. His greatness never made you feel uncomfortable, uneasy or insignificant. His humility effortlessly shone through. He would ask me, a spiritual infant (young enough to be his son), what to say in a speech, what managerial decision to make or what spiritual goal to set. He even asked me how to prepare for death. Obviously, he knew the answers, but he came down to your level and connected with love. He was my guru but treated me like a friend. A genius par excellence.

Dear Srutidharma, we miss you. Life is not the same. I should be sitting here crying, but then I hear you telling me, as you did on many occasions – *"Sutapa, if you don't learn to laugh, you cry!"* You taught us to laugh at the madness of the material world. *"Laugh and smile"* you said, *"then the weight of the world becomes lighter."* So, what to do… I'll remember your legacy, try to overcome my selfishness, contribute something to this glorious mission, remembering to smile and laugh along the way. *"Don't take the illusion too seriously"* you would say, *"here today, gone tomorrow."* Thank you for lending us the vision of eternity. Thank you for showing us that the saints are not just people of the past. Thank you for inspiring us to live a life of complete selflessness.

LOVING LIFE, EMBRACING DEATH (JUL 2021)

How many people can say they love life? How many people jump out of bed, inspired and enthused, on a mission that has captured their imagination? How many people are so driven that no amount of complexity or challenge could deflate them? Janakinath Das, aka JD, was a rare soul who exhibited such hunger for life.

He was a modern-day saint. An urban monk. You'd spot him in a baseball cap practicing new magic tricks, utilising technology and communicating profound spiritual truths through the lingo of the ghetto. JD was a powerhouse of spiritual energy - buzzing and bouncing from one mission to the next, conquering hearts with his simple smile and soft heart. His character exuded saintliness - tolerant, compassionate, friendly to all, without enemies and always peaceful. A childlike innocence that you couldn't imitate. No time to criticise or complain, always progressive and positive.

For him, life was a perpetual adventure. When he took up spirituality, became a monk and travelled the world with his backpack, it was an adventure. Later, when he was diagnosed with cancer, it was another adventure. When he was told he had three months to live, it was another adventure. When we talked about the arrangements for his own funeral, it was another adventure! In his final days, a medical opportunity arose. *"Boom!"* he said *"let's do it"*... it was yet another adventure, the last one of this life. JD left the world on the battlefield, embracing an unlikely prospect to turn his health around. He wanted to extend his time, not because he was scared of death, but because he was in love with life. Every moment was valuable because it brought beautiful opportunities to serve others.

JD loved life because he knew how to live life. When people struggled, he never judged them, ignored them, or remained indifferent, but rather extended a loving, helping hand. We'd have arguments - I'd make the 'clear' managerial decisions, but he'd make decisions which empowered, enthused, elevated and encouraged others. He showed me how a spiritualist should also be a kind human. When there was an opportunity to serve, he was never lazy, apathetic, or hesitant - he

Loving *Life*
Embracing *Death*

The story of the
Smiling Monk

Written by Sutapa Das

rolled up his sleeves and got stuck in, whatever the task. He knew the secret... he was a giver.

His life was hijacked by acute obstacles, but he responded with grace, resilience and inspired positivity. Those obstacles went from bad to worse to unthinkable. Month after month, year after year, the violent and aggressive reversals increased in intensity – 30 pills a day, relentless cycles of chemo, endless nights alone in hospital, loss of voice, physical incapacitation and inability to perform the most basic human functions. How such experiences can destroy someone! The heat kept rising, but JD's spirit outgrew it, absorbing everything in the blazing fire of his devotion. The last human freedom is the freedom to remain enthusiastic about life. A shining example for us all – he loved life because he knew how to live life.

JD wasn't just positive, but spiritually deep as well. He had implanted the most profound aspirations within his heart and was aiming for the North Star of spiritual perfection. Before the world went into lockdown he made one final trip to Vrindavana, the most holy of places. There he connected with the sweetness of transcendence and when he came back, he knew where he was aiming. He intensified this divine meditation till the final breath. I foolishly underestimated him!

O JD, who was always buzzing! Maybe now you're buzzing with the bees in the divine playground of God known as Goloka Vrindavana. Perhaps you're buzzing somewhere else in this universe, banging a drum in the electrifying movement of Sri Chaitanya-deva, cooking up a spiritual revolution of love. JD, my friend, you were miles ahead! You did it and I'm so happy for you. Hopefully we'll meet again for some more spiritual adventures and this time I'll follow you, so that I can learn to love life just as you did.

As we enter the post-Covid era, I'm back on the road. Well, more specifically in the air, flying from one terminal to another, making a small attempt to share spiritual wisdom far and wide. On a recent flight to Cairo, I managed to secure the sought-after emergency seat (when you're over 6ft tall that's a big deal!). Unfortunately, every perk comes at a price. Emergency seats tend to be where new-born babies also hang out... and often they're loud, crying, distressed babies! Today was one of those days – all the leg room in the world, but a screaming backing track to accompany it. This flight was going to require some... mind control!

I remembered Bhaktivedanta Swami, who taught us to desperately call out while chanting God's name, like a baby crying for the mother. That was the flash of inspiration! I reached for my prayer beads, closed my eyes and synchronised every bursting screech of the baby with a recitation of the mantra. I tried to internalise the cry and embody desperation in my meditation. Mysteriously therapeutic! I found my meditation growing in depth! Interestingly, the Bhagavad-gita's first chapter is entitled 'Visad-yoga' – the yoga of desperation. Real spiritual connection is triggered when a deep urgency burns within, driving one to venture beyond a space that's no longer habitable and satisfying.

Crying is a part of everyone's life, at all stages, in all settings. There is the cry of the *samsarika* (one entangled in material life) – a cry of frustration, born from the frantic and futile search for substance in the shadow. One sage sings of how the combined tears shed by the *samsarika* over lifetimes would comfortably fill multiple oceans. Then there is the cry of the *sadhaka* (a spiritual aspirant seeking divine connection) – a cry of desperation to become serious, sincere and spontaneously involved with the Supreme Person. Finally, there is the cry of the *siddha* (the perfected being) – a cry of spiritual intoxication, arising from the inexplicable joy of divine love in multifarious flavours and tastes.

There's no question of avoiding tears, but just a question of what one will cry for. One illustrious teacher explained how temples were actually 'crying schools' – unique places where one could channel the emotions of the heart to forge divine communion. Indeed, Srila Prabhupada mentions this is the last word in love – the capacity to cry for God. On that journey to Cairo, I prayed that the *samsarika* cry of the baby, would become the *sadhaka* cry of myself, so that one day it could be the *siddha* cry in the transcendent realm. A good lesson in the air.

___

GET REAL (MAY 2022)

The ability to communicate with clarity, power and authenticity is a priceless life skill. It's something I've often struggled with. Some convey their heart through art and song, some through the spoken word and others through practical action or personal exchange. In this period, some have found their voice over Zoom! For me, writing is, by far, my most authentic means of communication. It's expression and discovery, it encompasses truth and emotion, it's succinct yet multi-layered and it allows me to be alone and simultaneously with many. Writing allows for inner meditation and mass communication, it's impactful without being intrusive, it reverberates beyond the moment and it captures a snapshot of the inner world that the eyes can't access. For me, writing is a beautiful art of life that triggers deep self-development.

Beyond this, writing is where I get closest to being my real self – where I find my most authentic voice. The solitude helps immensely. My nature is to instinctively adjust to the people and places around me and while that can be a good thing, it can also inhibit an expression of the true self. We have to be sensitive without being superficial, to look for unity but not at the expense of honouring diversity. Life can often be a tug-of-war between appreciation and authenticity. We desire acknowledgment, approval and acceptance – looking good can easily take priority over living truthfully. We end up being someone we're not, putting up a facade and acting in a drama. We get the claps, the nods and pats on the back, but remain internally stifled.

To find true authenticity, however, we have to brave the initial feelings of unnaturalness. For many of us, it feels most natural when we conform to the prevailing set of social expectations and ideals. To leave that 'safe space' in search of true authenticity can be unnerving to say the least. Ralph Waldo Emerson said, *"To be yourself in a world that is constantly trying to make you something else is the greatest accomplishment."*

My conclusion is that deep divine connection is the only thing that can trigger genuine authenticity. When we're spiritually connected, the fulfilment and love we draw from our relationship with the Supreme allows us to function in this world without the need for recognition or praise, opening the doors to real authenticity. It's an incredibly powerful and revealing measure of our spiritual trajectory. If we're somewhat sensitive, our daily superficiality will scream out to us – a reminder that there's lots more work to do in becoming spiritually accomplished and divinely authentic.

DUST TO DUST (JUN 2022)

The holy River Ganga, descending from the transcendent realm and flowing through modern-day India, is a liquid flow of Divinity.

I recently journeyed there to disperse the ashes of two spiritual luminaries; a final farewell to these outstanding souls who moulded my life and touched my heart. It was a day of mixed emotions – a combination of sorrow and deep inspiration, vacancy but satisfaction, simultaneous feelings of separation and meeting as well. Spiritual relationships are unique, incorporating multifarious dimensions of emotion in paradoxical ways. No one word could sum it up. These individuals successfully penetrated my steel-framed heart – I felt conquered by their love.

I've always shied away from relationships. In my youth I read a book by one monastic who explained his cherished aspiration: to die without anyone knowing and anyone shedding a tear. Crazy as it sounds, the idea of 'social death' and total aloofness was extremely appealing to me! On my journey, however, the sweetness of the bhakti teachings began challenging my perceptions. At every step I noticed the emphasis on deep, heartfelt exchange. More than freedom from attachment, the goal was to become a slave of love. My 'inner-impersonlist' was exposed and I awoke to the realisation that relationships were the key to thriving in my spiritual journey – the kindness, encouragement and selfless exchange of love is our spiritual heartbeat. Without that we're living but dead.

The ashes disappeared into the flowing water, but the bond of friendship was still alive. What ultimately endures? A stream of reflections flooded my mind. When time runs out, I won't carry my prayer beads with me, but I will take the genuine taste I have for chanting the name of God. I won't carry my library with me, but I will take the realisation I've awakened within my heart from all that reading. I won't carry any positions or titles with me, but I will take the desire for service that I've developed. Our associates may not travel with us, but the heartfelt bonds based on selfless exchange will never be severed. On the bankside of the Ganga, I identified the daily question I need to ask myself – *what did I do today to invest in my eternal assets?*

Dispersing ashes in the river Ganga

ROYAL MINDSET (SEP 2022)

On 8th September 2022, at 3:10pm, Elizabeth II, Queen of the United Kingdom and the other Commonwealth realms and the longest-reigning British monarch, died of old age at Balmoral Castle in Scotland, at the age of 96. Ten years ago, I wrote about 'A Royal Meeting' with the Queen and today I'm meditating on 'A Royal Mindset' as I reflect on her life.

1) Satisfaction – born into a unique situation, the Queen not only accepted, but fully embraced the role she was destined for in life. She was satisfied and content with what Providence had ushered her into. Often, we deny, fight, lament or dream about how it could have been different. Today, I'm meditating on being fully satisfied with the role I'm meant to play in this world, whatever the challenges may be, confident that there is a higher arrangement behind it.

2) Sobriety – despite being so public, so powerful and surrounded by grandeur, the Queen maintained complete sobriety and integrity. Fame and fortune, success and spotlight, praise and position, can intoxicate and deviate like nothing else. The Queen, however, never became overwhelmed or overpowered. Today I'm meditating on how to remain grounded, even when everything around us becomes bigger, bolder and brighter.

3) Steadiness - at today's funeral the Archbishop commented: *"Her Late Majesty famously declared on a 21st birthday broadcast that her whole life would be dedicated to serving the Nation and Commonwealth. Rarely has such a promise been so well kept!"* That unshakeable steadiness is something to aspire for. I'm meditating on how I became a monk when I was 21. Now I need to dig deeper and find that same commitment and steadiness to honour my vows till the end with grace, devotion and resilience. How beautiful that would be.

Meeting the Queen at Lambeth Palace

CONSCIOUS CHANGEMAKERS (SEP 2022)

A recent dialogue at the Cambridge University Divinity School impelled me to dig a little deeper. With the world in fresh disarray, the crowd was on top-form in firing doubts and suspicions about what spirituality could bring to the table. Many opined that spiritualists can't meaningfully engage with the world as tangible changemakers since they are inherently too 'other worldly.' Here were the three top arguments:

Observing Life

Doubt: Spiritualists tend to prioritise their inner life of prayer and meditation over practical and tangible service to humanity.

My response: Global revolutions begin with personal resolutions and thus our external contribution cannot be divorced from our inner life. Powerful engagement with the world begins with transforming the ecology of our own heart. If we're not living representations of the character, values and saintly qualities we seek to share with the world, how much impact can we really have? The core solution to humanity's problems is an upliftment of consciousness, deeper sensitivity and a genuine vision of spiritual unity. The humble spiritualists trigger that revolution of consciousness from the inside out. They see themselves as doctors and patients simultaneously – working for the world and also working on themselves.

Doubt: Spiritualists see the world as hard-wired for suffering and their pessimism in comprehensively solving global problems reinforces those same problems.

My Response: Not being in full control doesn't mean we can't make a difference. Understanding that the world will never be perfect actually empowers our efforts to contribute, rescuing us from any frustration arising from unrealistic expectations. Spiritualists enthusiastically help with practical solutions, but they take it a step further, knowing that those solutions have their limitations. Thus, they also deliver transformational spiritual wisdom, teaching people the art of how to develop inner immunity despite being surrounded by chaos. They endeavour to improve the 'outside' but put the emphasis on empowering the 'inside.'

Doubt: Spiritualists develop a detachment from the world that lacks the emotional involvement to make a heartfelt difference.

My Response: The most powerful change-maker is the one who seeks

With various representatives at Cambridge University

no personal benefit from it. US president, Harry Truman, summed it up when he said, *"It's amazing what you can accomplish when you don't care who gets the credit."* In that sense, the detachment of the spiritualist generates a selflessness that translates into incredible levels of uninterrupted service. Immature and misapplied detachment leads to heartlessness, but true detachment can foster the deepest sentiments of kindness and compassion since ego has been eliminated from the equation.

The world needs conscious changemakers - spiritual changemakers. As Einstein famously said, *"You can't solve problems with the same type of thinking that created them."*

COVID-19

If you've never experienced the danger of war, the agony of imprisonment or torture, or the horrible pangs of starvation, then you are luckier than 500 million people for whom this is a daily reality. Behind the pleasant veneer, lies an extremely volatile and violent world. Most of us, however, only ever perceive that in the form of a television report about some atrocity on the other side of the world.

In 2020, however, we all caught a glimpse of that volatility when the Covid-19 Pandemic broke out. The UK was one of the hardest hit places and our spiritual community was directly impacted with hundreds of casualties. Life changed overnight. A bustling temple turned into a quiet monastery and the resident monks became truly recluse for the first time in their life. With social distancing, the online platforms became the new meeting place. In that period, there was lots of time to think, reflect and recalibrate life. It was a revealing time. Here, I share some of my musings through that unprecedented event.

COVID TO KOVIDA (MAR 2020)

Latest: Covid-19 has hit 200,000 cases worldwide, triggering over 8,000 deaths.

In Sanskrit, the word *kovida* refers to one who is intelligent, wise and philosophically inclined. To appropriately respond to Covid, we each have to become *kovida*. Positive affirmations, optimistic propaganda and comforting words are appreciated... but only go so far. We need spiritual insight to decode this mysterious global event.

When dealing with the news of the world we can go to extremes. Some people lose themselves in the barrage of information that gushes through and become *intimidated* by the whole situation, feeling powerless and hopeless. Others disconnect themselves totally and become *indifferent*, feeling it better to remain in their own bubble away from the chaos. The middle-way, however, would be to remain *informed*, and try to view global events and experiences through a spiritual lens.

It may be time to take a break from reading endless articles and watching every other newsflash. We pretty much know what's happening and tiny details here and there don't really change the landscape. Instead of getting bogged down into the crazy world of panic, perhaps we could open up to the bigger picture of life. Close observation will reveal an incredible correlation between what's written in ancient wisdom texts and what we see before our eyes. If we pause for a moment and digest the deeper lessons that are surfacing, we may find that Covid ushers us into a fresh new reality, individually and globally.

Find opportunities in problems.

Latest: Millions of people are lying low to limit the spread of Covid-19. Self-isolation and social distancing, they say, will help curb the crisis. Next problem: how do you cope with being cooped up for days on end? How do we use this time wisely?

Consider the three biggest reasons why people don't experience growth in their life – they are too busy, too proud or too comfortable. We're falling short of our potential. Could government-enforced self-isolation be a solution in disguise?

Thanks to Covid-19 we have time on our hands. In the daily treadmill, the endless issues and relentless demands of functional life suck up all our waking hours. Now we're forced into somewhat of a lockdown – a situation that facilitates reflection, planning, questioning and the crafting of a more conscious direction in life. We'd never free up that time ourselves, so here it is handed to us on a silver platter.

Thanks to Covid-19 our weaknesses have been exposed. The Pandemic has humbled us. The stress, insecurity and uncertainty make us realise we're not as flawless as we thought. The media reports showing self-centredness in pursuance of self-preservation are astonishing! It has become evidently obvious that some inner engineering needs to go on. The two most revealing times in life come when we are in solitude and when we are in stress. How we act in those times reveals what's really inside.

Thanks to Covid-19 we've ignited some urgency. The last two weeks are a wake-up call to not take things for granted. Comfort is a silent killer and complacency is our middle name. We never thought the situation could become so acute, so quickly. Thank you for blowing our misconceptions and reminding us that time is precious and life is volatile. Harsh realities help reinstate clarity and perspective into every aspect of our life.

Apprehensive about self-isolation? Don't be. Create a vision, make a plan, build a schedule and use this time ingeniously. It may never come again. We'll look back at this strange time and realise how valuable it was.

Find opportunities in problems.

COVID CONTRADICTIONS (MAR 2020)

Someone asked me if we should pray for the protection of our loved ones – of course we should! But it got me thinking...

We have a deep fear about losing family and friends...

But are we as worried about how we relate to them while they're alive?

We have a deep fear of disease and illness...

But are we as concerned about bad diet and no exercise when we're healthy?

We have a deep fear that we'll lose our freedom...

But are we fussed about our daily laziness, procrastination and time-wasting?

We have a deep fear of death...

But are we bothered about living a meaningless life?

Ironic, isn't it? We're perpetually fearful about what we'll lose but neglect it on a daily basis when we have it. Though I feel like culprit number one, I'm hopeful that there is still some time to rectify the situation. Maybe Covid-19 will overturn our contradictory existence

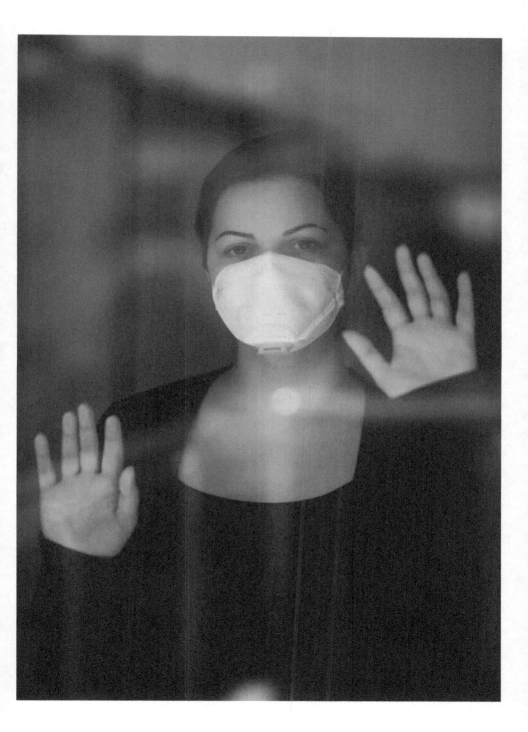

so that instead of worrying about what may be in the future, we get focused on what we should do in the here and now.

Find opportunities in problems.

KOVIDA COMPASS ^(MAR 2020)

The word *kovida* appears in a celebrated verse from the Srimad-Bhagavatam:

"Those who are intelligent and philosophically inclined (kovida) should endeavour for that which is beyond the material world. Happiness derived from material sources is obtained automatically, just as in course of time we obtain miseries even though we do not desire them." (Paraphrased, S.B. 1.5.18)

Just as Covid-19 appeared without any invitation, our allotted material happiness, prosperity and well-being automatically appears according to the karmic cycle. That's not to say we don't endeavour determinedly and act dutifully, but it does mean we understand that, on the material level, whatever will be, will be - *que sera sera*. This being the case, to navigate the course of life, which is riddled with surprises beyond our control, we need a spiritual compass - a *kovida* compass?

1) Adjust your expectation - false expectations will bring great frustrations. We're not designed to control the world, so don't be surprised when things don't go to plan. If something can go wrong, it will - expect the unexpected. Disempowering? Not really, because the good news is that happiness is not outside of us. Contentment in life is not based on controlling the external world, but rather on conquering the inner world. We don't have to wait for a change around us to find peace within us.

2) Accept your situation – every external situation can bring internal growth. Properly digested experiences will nourish us with strength, wisdom, humility and powerful insight. The unexpected occurrences are part of a master plan to reconfigure our consciousness. We only have to learn some acceptance and stop fighting, denying, or cursing a situation. Our gut reaction is to blame others, blame the stars, blame the government or blame God. In the blame game, however, we end up staying the same.

3) Aspire for connection – in the midst of unpredictability and the rollercoaster ride of life, we need a permanent anchor. By rooting ourselves in the spiritual reality, we learn to view life's occurrences on the backdrop of eternity. Come what may, success or failure, fortune or frustration, highs or lows, our spiritual status remains unharmed and untouched. This connection is known as yoga, a process which reconnects us to the eternal HQ. In the world but not of it.

Let the mantra become part of you: *adjust your expectation, accept your situation, and aspire for connection.*

Find opportunities in problems.

RESTRICTED FREEDOM (MAR 2020)

Latest: UK Lockdown intensifies – no social visits, no whimsical shopping, no unnecessary trading, no avoidable travelling, no public gatherings. Everything will be police-enforced.

We've seemingly lost our freedom, but, have we? Here are some points for your consideration:

When 'freedom' means that everything is so available that we become familiar and complacent, what's the benefit? If 'restriction' generates an appreciation and gratitude of what we've taken for granted all these years, where's the loss?

When 'freedom' means we act and speak unrestrictedly, oblivious to the ramifications, what's the benefit? If 'restriction' creates the space to exercise our freedom to THINK, helping us become sensitive and aware, where's the loss?

When 'freedom' means we're bombarded by so many things that we can't focus on anything, what's the benefit? If 'restriction' allows us to concentrate on a few things and do them well, where's the loss?

When 'freedom' means we become imperceptibly dependent on comforts and facilities for our sanity, what's the benefit? If 'restriction' helps one develop the wealth of detachment from temporary arrangements which are bound for dissolution, where's the loss?

When 'freedom' means we're so 'close' to people that we fail to deeply connect, what's the benefit? If 'restriction' creates a physical separation that sparks more conscious and meaningful interaction, where's the loss?

Misused 'freedom' actually limits our life. Utilised 'restriction' can open the doors to real freedom. Freedom, my friends, is defined by something way deeper than governmental laws. Consciousness creates reality.

Find Opportunities in Problems.

Covid-19 lockdown in the Monastery

LESSONS ON THE ROAD

Every December, the monks travel up and down the country connecting with as many souls as humanly possible. The high streets, city centres, bustling markets and urban hubs become their second home as they descend to ground reality, meeting the people, stimulating inquisitiveness and sharing wisdom that breathes. It's quite a task to intercept someone in their tracks, weave beyond the complex myriad of thoughts, penetrate the bubble of their life and begin a dialogue about deeper topics. Some people naturally tune in, while others are sceptical, uninterested and otherwise-engaged. Each to his own, after all, everyone is on a unique journey.

In these times, mystical, magical, memorable and moving things happen. It often feels like a transcendental drama where providential participation is palpable and recurrent. This is street-spirituality and what I call the 'School of Life' – hands-on training in resilience, sensitivity, compassion, communication and humility. Things you don't necessarily learn in the classroom. Over the last twenty years I have learnt so many lessons on the road. It's the place where book wisdom comes alive.

COLD SHOWERS (DEC 2019)

It's Monday morning and it's cold, wet and windy. It's time to face the world. It's another day on book distribution!

I remember returning from my first day on book distribution and being advised to do the unthinkable – *"Go and have a cold shower!"* What! I'd already been standing in the freezing cold all day! The logic was that a warm shower cleanses your physical body, but a cold shower cleanses your subtle body – all the negative energy that we absorb from a day in the urban jungle is cleansed away by cooling waters. After an intense bout of mental warfare, I did it and it actually felt amazing (but only after it was finished!). I've never seen the scientific evidence for it, but you can definitely perceive the purifying effect. The same person told me that book distribution was like a cold shower. In fact, he said, progressive life is full of cold showers – doing things which, in the beginning, are uncomfortable, but eventually bring a great wealth. Building momentum takes bucket loads of energy, but once you're flowing, it's effortless and enlivening.

Upon reflection, I see a crystal-clear correlation in my life. The best things I ever did were often the very things I passionately resisted in the beginning. The things I avoided, argued against and convinced myself were unnecessary – those were the things that brought me the invaluable jewels of growth. It's ironic and scary at the same time. It means I'll probably have to do a whole bunch of other uncomfortable things in order to experience the entirety of what life can be. The lesson is loud and clear: those who are convenience-focused are experience-starved. *But why are the best things so hard to do? Why are good habits difficult to form? Why are bad habits formed so effortlessly? Why aren't we able to spontaneously embrace the things that are so beneficial to us? Who made the system like this?* It seems as though someone has stacked the odds against us.

The truth is that our mindset and consciousness make it all topsy-turvy. Because we are incorrectly 'inclined,' we are flowing in the wrong direction and all the beneficial things feel difficult and unnatural. In material consciousness, our habits, behaviours, thoughts and desires naturally drift towards the damaging. When we re-engineer our consciousness and correct our 'inclination' then everything flows naturally towards the positive and progressive. That, however, takes time, effort, determination and patience. Therefore, the biggest battle of the day is the battle over our own mind. If we win that one, we become empowered in the process of transformation and open the doors to a whole new world. *Ready for another cold shower?*

CHEATERS TO TEACHERS (DEC 2019)

You have a 20-second window to make an impression. Someone stops, you size them up, put in a spiritual pitch, something interesting, inspirational and endearing and wait for a reaction – hit, miss or blank... anything could happen! What's for sure, is that people are perceptive (more than we may think). They can sniff out any sense of superficiality, selfish motive, self-righteousness or insecurity within moments. Sometimes they make it known to you and boy is that humbling! At other times they stay quiet, but it leaves an impression on them. People may forget what you say, but they'll never forget how you made them feel. One striking life lesson on the road is that teachers can't be cheaters. We have to live and breathe what we seek to share, because when we communicate, we are not just transmitting the perceptible, but the subtle as well. That invisible element, as we've all experienced, penetrates deeper.

Overcoming the cheating mentality is not easy. The sages explain that we each have four defects – the potential to fall into illusion (*pramada*), the disability of imperfect senses (*karanapatava*), a propensity to commit mistakes (*bhrama*) and the mentality of cheating (*vipralipsa*). From one perspective they are all interlinked. Because we fall under illusion, we receive a body with imperfect senses. Because we have imperfect senses, we often make mistakes. Because we commit mistakes, we end up cheating to 'save our face.' Whilst the first three are somewhat beyond our control at the present time, the fourth is definitely not. To be straightforward and honest, especially when we make mistakes, is the sign of sincerity, and that disposition is perhaps one of the most important factors in spiritual progress.

In life, weakness is acceptable, but cheating is definitely not. When we present ourselves in a dishonest way, it's neither satisfying, nor is it sustainable, nor will it support our spiritual aspirations. When confronted with our shortcomings, if we cover them up, brush them under the carpet, and lock them in the closet, we'll probably find they come back to haunt us down the line. We have to deal with the real. *But shouldn't we act pure to become pure? If I'm proud, shouldn't I atleast act humble in order to awaken that true humility? Isn't some level of pretending required on the progressive spiritual path? Don't we have to 'fake it till we make it'?* Yes. There is truth in that. Yet, I often remind myself:

Don't fake it so much that you think you've made it.

Don't fake it simply to convince others that you've made it.

Don't fake it without a deep and sincere desire to make it.

Otherwise, in faking it, you'll end up breaking it.

"*Cheating and weakness are two separate things. Persons devoid of a cheating propensity achieve perfection in life, but a cheater is never successful. Vaisnavism is another name for simplicity... Sincere persons can be weak, but they are not cheaters. Cheaters say something but do something else. Weak people are embarrassed by their defects, whereas cheaters are maddened by their achievements." (Bhaktisiddhanta Saraswati Thakur)*

GIVE ME HOPE (DEC 2019)

The streets of the UK are host to nearly a quarter of a million homeless people. Today he sits on the sidewalk, in minus degree temperatures, holding a ragged sign which reads *"Give me hope."* It's a familiar sight that I've become somewhat desensitised to; I don't think I can ever truly understand his situation. Seeing him sleeping rough, a few people throw in some coins, another person gifts him a Costa coffee, while an occasional passer-by stops to share some comforting words.

All nice gestures. But, my heart says, what he really needs is hope. In that sense we are all beggars – we all need hope. Without the conviction of a brighter future what drives us to continue on in life? Hope fuels our hunger for life, and is perhaps our most precious asset. If we have that, everything else can be awakened.

The raw reality is that on the material level, there is no hope. There may be positive thoughts, determined affirmations, optimistic plans and elaborate arrangements, but it all eventually crumbles away as the ruthless laws of nature indiscriminately take over. True hope can only come from deep spirituality. That transcendent dimension brings a deeper purpose, Divine presence and profound empowerment that shifts our consciousness entirely. A mentor once described the spiritual reality as the realm of 'unlimited possibility.' He told me that if I'm patient, I'll witness how divine plans are way better than our cherished dreams. I was moved. At the time it was hope-giving and over time I've realised the weight of that statement. There is more beyond our mind, beyond our life and beyond our world. When we are awakened to that, we live life, full of hope.

Undeserving as I am, I've been blessed with teachers and friends who filled my life with hope. They gave me spiritual vision and generous infusions of encouragement at every step. I can't believe anyone who says they are self-made – we stand tall because we stand on the shoulders of our predecessors. It's a humbling thought and now I realise that perhaps the greatest gift we can share with someone is the gift of spiritual hope. It reminded me of the story of two prime ministers. After meeting the first, you left the room thinking *"that man is wonderful!"* After meeting the second, you left the room thinking *"he is wonderful and I could also do something wonderful!"* That is the difference between a *good* friend and a *great* friend – the *great* give encouragement, empowerment and hope. They give the vision of a brighter future. May we encounter such great souls again and again and may we share the hope they give us with many others. As Nelson Mandela reminded us, *"May our life choices reflect our hopes, not our fears."*

GREAT EXPECTATIONS (DEC 2019)

Competition is so engrained in modern culture. In a variety of spheres, spiritual one's included, your performance, proficiency and position is in the spotlight and it feels like everyone is watching, sizing you up. For some it's entirely unnerving, for others it's positively motivating. Some of us run a mile and others relish the challenge. To a greater or lesser extent, we are all affected in some way. Our life is so much shaped by the expectations of those around us. And how many expectations there are, many of which are diametrically opposed! *How do we harness pressure and attention to create growth? How do we avoid becoming overwhelmed and overburdened? How do we keep everyone happy? Is it humanly possible to live up to all of these expectations and should we even try?*

We have to be careful not to lose ourselves in the voices of the world. Thomas Cooley writes: *"I am not who you think I am; I am not who I think I am; I am who I think you think I am!"* If you didn't get that, try reading it again. If it's still unclear, don't worry – the essential point is that many of us have become hijacked by expectations and disconnected from our authentic self. Life is packed with a host of pressures from family, friends, society and the media to be a certain type of person. In the mad rush to meet all those demands we're left with little scope to pursue our own calling. In the attempt to satisfy everyone, we could end up bitter and miserable. After all, *we* have to live our life and to do that we have to love our life.

But let's not go to an extreme. There is more to life than just doing what *we* want. Pleasing those around us, sacrificing our own plans for a higher cause and learning to be flexible to feedback also moulds our spiritual character. The expectations of others can be positively empowering. It's a unique gift to have someone in our life who has a greater vision for us than we could have come up with ourselves. Since well-wishers can open us up to a world we never knew existed we should avoid the extreme of shying away from all expectations. The key is to respect everyone, but to embrace the expectations of certain individuals with more seriousness. If you try to please everyone you'll end up pleasing no one. Those who know you, feel for you and can actually help you (on a practical and spiritual level) – their expectations count for more. Their expectations will be realistic, realised and truly rewarding. In their words of expectation comes the empowerment to meet those expectations, and our lives thus become a transcendental drama. We must learn the art of riding the fast-flowing river of expectations and avoid drowning in it.

INTENSITY (DEC 2019)

Yesterday I parked my book box outside the festive merry-go-round. From morning to evening I heard the same 4-song playlist over and over again. These jingles hijack your mind! By the end of the day, I found myself singing the line, *"I wish it could be Christmas everydaaay,"* in between meeting people! I thought about this special time of year when we make an extra effort to reach out. *What if every month would be like this month? What if every day was a Book Marathon day?*

We've travelled over 2000 miles in 25 days, up and down the country, meeting thousands of people and handing out thousands of books. The marathon is coming to an end. Exhilarating but exhausting. A part of me would like it to go on and on, and another part of me is dying for a break! Without doubt, there is one quality that makes this month incredibly special – intensity! We eat, sleep and breathe with one single meditation in mind. In intensity there's no time for distractions and diversions. In intensity we forget material conceptions and go beyond self-imposed limitations. In intensity we experience an absorbed spirituality that bursts with excitement, realisation and magical experiences. In intensity we gain a glimpse of transcendence. The beautiful Bhagavatam thus recommends we tread the spiritual path with great... intensity (*tivrena bhakti-yogena*).

Intensity, however, is not easy to come by. Most of us are not bad spiritual practitioners, but just casual ones. We're strict on a few things and loose on a lot more. We take a bit of this, add bit of that, avoid the uncomfortable, blend it together with half-hearted effort and pray it's the recipe for enlightenment. Doesn't sound promising. Without intensity, how will we ever have a breakthrough in spiritual experience? Yet we shy away from it. Maybe we're afraid we can't sustain it? Maybe we're scared that we'll miss out on something? Maybe we observe others and veer towards the lowest common denominator? Maybe we just don't have the conviction to put that much of our heart into it? For some, intensity sounds like insanity.

Today, my heart told me that intensity means integrity. When our actions align with our aspirations, we live a life of integrity. If we've actually registered the loftiness of our purpose, the reality of our situation and the urgency of time, then intensity will naturally manifest in our actions. There is so much to do. There's no time to lose! Intensity is not only for a day or a month or a year. Intensity has to become a thread throughout our lives. As a month of intensity concludes, I'm contemplating what form that intensity will take for the coming year.

We have to discover an intensity that fits with our personality, so we can maintain a consistency that will blossom our spirituality.

You may have seen the freezing child experiment. If not, take a look on YouTube and see just how apathetic we can be. More unnerving than the video was the introspection it triggered within me. *If I walked past a freezing child in the street, would I stop to help?* Of course, we could give a variety of excuses to justify why not to – it's not practical, it could be a hoax, life is busy. The critical question, however, is the level of human sensibility we embody. As a kid, I religiously avoided trips into Central London because the sight of homeless people was too uncomfortable. Later on, as a university student, I had to live in London, and it became a daily sight – I became desensitised and learnt to live with it. *Is that acceptable? Is it good to be able to comfortably live with the pain of others?* Nowadays I feel that kind of apathy is a major block to my spiritual progression.

Spirituality is a journey from selfishness to selflessness. Somewhere along the road we have to develop sensitivity, because without it, selflessness is never born. The insensitive see other people suffering, but it doesn't really register or move their heart – this is *apathy*. The desensitised genuinely pity other people's suffering from a distance but learn to live with it – this is *sympathy*. When we manage to resensitise ourselves, however, we look upon other people's suffering and feel impelled to act and assist – this is *empathy*. In Sanskrit, a true spiritualist is known as *para dukkha dukhi*, or one who feels another's pain to be their own. Scriptures are replete with stories of great souls who went above and beyond the call of duty to free others from their troubles.

I have enough of my own problems to deal with! How can I take the weight of the world on my shoulders? Won't this lead to compassion fatigue? Can we really make a difference anyway? No doubt, we have to be practical – self-care and self-compassion are foundational.

Unless we're well situated how can we really help others? That said, taking care of ourselves is not the success of life, because we exist to make a beautiful contribution to the world and the souls in it. That opportunity to serve is what gives life to our years on this planet.

A guru and his disciple were walking along a coastline where thousands of shellfish had been washed ashore. Seeing them struggling, the guru periodically threw one in as he paced the ocean front. Seeing the sheer numbers of struggling fish, the disciple questioned whether his attempts would really make a difference. *"It will make a difference to THAT particular fish"* the guru said. The disciple realised that in the statistics, he had lost his sensitivity... perhaps the story of our life. From apathy, to sympathy, to empathy. Casting out insensitivity, going beyond de-sensitivity and ultimately becoming re-sensitised. This is the journey of spiritual life. After all, only a sensitive heart can experience the magical depths of spiritual connection, emotion and devotion.

PRISONERS OF THE PAST (DEC 2022)

Festive periods usually highlight how much our lives have changed, triggering memories and nostalgia of how it used to be. People have come and gone, relationships redefined, fortunes have swung, lifestyles transformed. Everyone wanders to the past – so many events, experiences and emotions that have made us who we are today. To think of the past is natural. To live in the past, however, is nonsensical. Mark the difference. The past can be instructive and inspiring, but also haunting and limiting. Some enter that space and never find their way out. A painful past captures many, confining us into the role of a victim, holding on to wrongdoings and imprisoned by bitterness, hurt and regret. We demand explanations, justifications, rationalisations –

but would those 'answers' really pacify the heart anyway? Ironically, other people become prisoners of nostalgia. They constantly reminisce about the 'good old times,' reliving sweet memories and wishing they could turn back the clock. They psychologically block themselves from further discovery, mournful that it will never be the same again. In the bitter-sweet symphony of life, it's so easy to become a prisoner of the past.

The Bhagavad-gita identifies four levels of vision – seeing through the senses, the sentiments, the scriptures and the soul. The first two levels of vision are what 99.9% of people have become accustomed to. They see with their physical eyes and interpret through their memories, mindset and mood. Though this vision seems natural and automatic, it lacks creativity and depth – fresh perspectives, empowering insights and alternative revelations rarely arise from it. When we view life

through our senses and sentiments we're confined in the small world of our own limited human perceptions. This vision doesn't introduce us to new possibilities, and is therefore much more likely to imprison us in the past. We need to find a gateway, portal and passage to higher vision.

Enter the ancient books of wisdom – not just ink and paper, but the potentiality of a whole new life. Accessing the timeless words of the sages, saints and Supreme intelligence, lends one the possibility to start seeing the world through scripture and eventually, through the eyes of the soul. In reality, we're not human beings having a spiritual experience, but rather spiritual beings having a human experience. Wisdom lifts us to this elevated vantage point, offering profound perspective and bringing everything back into perfect clarity. We acknowledge the past but view it from a detached perspective above our own emotions. Beyond that, we see an extraordinary future – so much beauty in the life yet to unfold. We see the prospect of where our journey is taking us and feel inspired to reach it. When we open our eyes to the spiritual potentiality before us, a beautiful dream on the horizon, there is no hesitancy in letting go of the past, no point in constantly looking back.

Friends, let us venture beyond the senses and sentiment and learn to see through the scriptures and the soul. One fine day, we'll fully embody the vision of eternity and enter the world of unlimited possibility... onwards and upwards.

TAKE A NO IN STYLE (DEC 2022)

Today we're attempting to intercept a few souls from the gushing human river flow. *"No, I'm not interested... No, I don't believe in God... No, I don't read books... No, I'm as broke as a joke!"* No, No, No! Once,

I asked someone to spare a few moments for a quick conversation – *"No, I don't have time."* He carried on walking, *"But have you ever questioned life?"* – *"No, I don't have time."* As he faded into the distance I called out, *"No worries, have a good day"* – *"No I don't have time!"* It's ironic. In that moment I wanted to remind him that some things in life are so critical (our happiness included) that it's not about having time, it's about making time. Dealing with *"no's,"* however, is a part of the game. We often become despondent, deflated and demotivated, and thus a mentor once told me – *"learn to take a no in style!"* It was interesting. Later on I felt as though that was the key to life itself.

In life, we don't always get what we want. In life, people don't reciprocate with us in the ways we'd expect. In life, our plans are often derailed and everything from the weather to world politics seems stacked against us. Sometimes the heart says yes, but the body says no. Other times, your closest family and friends refuse to support. How do we respond to the *"no's"* of life? Firstly, we have to appreciate that the *"no's"* are a necessary part of life – if we were gifted everything on a plate we'd likely be in big trouble. St Teresa of Avila said, *"More tears were shed from prayers that were answered than ones that went unanswered."* Secondly, that *"no"* helps us to develop character, dig a little deeper and become more introspective and sensitive. Those refusals build us up. Thirdly, the *"no"* is designed to redirect us to a bigger *"yes."* We have to tune into providence's master plan, because every time one door closes, multiple others open.

Today I received one hour of *"no's"* in a row. It was pretty intense and I reminded myself – *"learn to take a 'no' in style."* Keep smiling, stay enthusiastic, do your best and be positive, knowing that at any moment everything could change. And it did, somehow or other. All's well that ends well. Now I just need to reproduce that graceful resilience in the game of life. Learn to take a *"no"* in style.

MYSTICAL INDIA

India is the land of extremes. You can ascend to the altitudes of the Himalayan mountains and then descend to the dry, scorching deserts. There is drought and monsoon, severe poverty and unimaginable opulence, breath-taking beauty and heart-breaking pollution, chaos and serenity, courtesy and rudeness. It all exists side-by-side, alternating with the blink of an eye. The most mystical extreme is that India spans material to spiritual - geographically situated in the physical dimension, yet packed with innumerable tirthas, or mystical portals, which connect one to the transcendent reality.

I first visited Vrindavana in 2002. After that trip, I didn't return for eight years. When my spiritual teacher heard that he told me I was a ghost – living but not really living! He encouraged me to reconnect and spend regular time there for spiritual rejuvenation and inner evolution. In 2010, I started visiting Vrindavana for one month every year. It was a time to disconnect, not just from technology and busyness, but also from the identities and social positions we wear in this world. In Vrindavana those things disappear as we become spiritual beggars, desperately searching for jewels of spiritual inspiration that can carry us forward.

NOWHERE TO HIDE (JAN 2018)

Back in Vrindavana by some good fortune. It's a relief, an inspiration, but simultaneously a daunting challenge as well. Here there's no other business, save and except cultivating a deeper spiritual connection. All the space and time in the world and not an excuse in sight. Back in London I can hide behind day-to-day responsibilities, practical demands, so-called achievements and given abilities, keeping busy and convincing myself that the journey is surely moving forward. Surrounded by a plethora of convenient justifications, we often avoid doing the internal soul-searching required for any sincere spiritualist. It's possible to continue on for years without consciously gauging our actual level of spiritual absorption and genuine devotional substance. But now there's nowhere to hide. It's me, Krishna, my books, my beads, lots of time to think and the unique atmosphere of Vrindavana to inspire the connection.

They say your life is out of balance when you suddenly end up with some free time and you just don't know what to do with yourself. It's existentially unnerving. Well, it sometimes feels like that when you come to the holy places in an off-peak time, with no 'business,' no meetings and no particular agenda in mind. The holy places proofread your devotion. We enter these sacred boundaries thinking we have developed so much, a long list of achievements, qualifications and devotional attributes. After a few days, however, you feel like the substance is probably significantly less. The proof-reader has edited down the story of our spiritual life, omitting all the waffle and superficiality.

It's humbling. A challenge, however, is also the greatest opportunity. It's a healthy jolt to get you back on track. Vrindavana hones you in to remember the essence of life. It's the place where the saints and sages documented, discussed and demonstrated the zenith of spiritual

purity. Yesterday I visited the Radha Damodar temple, where Srila Prabhupada spent many beautiful years living as a lone mendicant. During his time here, he told of a Bengali widow who unfailingly walked to the Yamuna River every morning, promptly returning with a pot of sacred water for the service of the Deities. Sometimes he would open the temple gate for her, intently observing her demeanour. Reflecting on her devotion, he said she would surely attain spiritual perfection in this very life. Her entrance to eternity guaranteed, for her heart was completely devoid of selfishness and pretention. A natural devotion from deep within. Simple as that. It's a reality check indeed. *When, oh when?*

OPEN DOORS OPEN HEARTS (JAN 2018)

Vrindavana has an open-door policy. Just take a stroll around the village lanes and someone will invite you in for a meal somewhere. It's happened to me three days in a row so far. In bygone ages, householders would loudly call for any hungry person in the vicinity before taking their own lunch. Such a beautiful culture. Sages would randomly drop by and offer gracious words of wisdom, people would liberally share things with their neighbours and children would freely run from home to home without any restrictions. It's a stark contrast to our modern world, which is closed up and shut tight. Nobody enters our fortress, with top notch surveillance and guard dogs to make sure. Hardly anyone ventures out, too busy watching TV or surfing the net. Locked into our small worlds, lacking genuine human interaction and becoming more and more isolated as the days pass by.

Today I reflected on how open doors create open hearts. The trends of society fashion the culture of an individual. Where people grow up with the open-door ethos, they naturally tend towards more open-heartedness – interested to hear the voice of others, ready to share their own thoughts and able to consciously interact with sensitivity and empathy. Such open-hearted exchange is at the very heart of spirituality. The modern world, however, with its closed-door policy, has inevitably crafted closed hearts. People are becoming socially awkward; impersonal, defensive, insensitive and selfish in their outlook. Our world shrinks when we close our doors and our worldview shrinks when we close our hearts. In these few days, people have said and done things for me that I would never have thought of doing for anyone else. It's touching but humbling and embarrassing at the same time. Another resounding reminder of the need to become more open-hearted.

How nice it would be if I could genuinely appreciate others, remembering how many people generously encourage me every single day. Maybe I could be more empathetic, balancing strength with sensitivity, recollecting the tireless mentors who patiently moulded and nurtured me despite my stubbornness. Considering how many selfless acts I was the recipient of, I wonder when I'll rid myself of my calculative mentality and embrace the joy of sacrificing to serve others. How relationships would transform if I was open-hearted enough to park my nit-picking judgemental attitude and give people the benefit of the doubt. What about if I could let go and forgive, instead of bottling things up and holding grudges. I'm living in anticipation of the day when I'll let cynicism and scepticism slide and exude genuine positivity and optimism. Oh Vrindavana, demolish the lock of impersonalism, slide back the bolt of miserliness, turn down the latch of insensitivity and reopen the doors of my heart so I can enter the world of selfless spiritual exchange.

DISCOVERING DISCOMFORT (JAN 2018)

Whether it's the coldest pre-dawn hours of winter, or the staggering heat of May and June, the external conditions in Vrindavana are far from perfect. Along with the climatic attacks, there is noise, pollution, decrepit infrastructure... whatever you do and however you try, Vrindavana inevitably ushers you into some level of austerity. When hardships come, however, people here have learnt to grit their teeth, accept it with a smile and carry on with enthusiasm. Some even actively embrace discomfort to deepen their spirituality. Either way, accepting it, or embracing it, austerity is a staple part of Vrindavana life. It's a paradigm diametrically opposed to the 'developed world,' where we impulsively do anything and everything to escape austerity and discomfort. The notion of tolerating difficulty is fast disappearing from the modern dictionary.

The name *'Sutapa'* denotes *'The person who performs great austerity.'* Thankfully I was given the name *'Sutapa Das,'* denoting the **servant** of such illustrious personalities. That was a lifesaver indeed. My capacity for voluntary hardship definitely has its limits. Observing the ascetic lifestyle of Vrindavana's residents, however, is giving me a different perspective. If we perennially avoid discomfort and difficulty, frantically searching for immediate adjustments and relief, we'll simply end up suffering more. Why so?

Firstly, on a physical level it's only a matter of time before we face certain hardships that we can't side-step. If we've inadvertently cemented ourselves into an expectation that we can mitigate and avoid discomfort, we'll find ourselves disturbed, frustrated and depressed when we encounter life's inescapable difficulties. Secondly, on a mental level, voluntarily accepting austerity trains you to elevate your consciousness to something higher in order to deal with the discomfort. If we've never practiced that art and never achieved that

elevation, we'll never really tune in to the sacred space of sanctuary beyond the inevitable material chaos. Thus, voluntary acceptance of hardship, what we call austerity, is something like a vaccination. It's an intentional acceptance of pain, that eventually saves you from a whole lot more.

While the whole world may pity the 'unfortunate' hardships that spiritualists in holy places undergo, they may not realise that these personalities are several steps ahead of the game. They're aware that this world is wired to be uncomfortable and they know the preparation required to digest that inevitable reality. Vrindavana is therefore known as *tapo-bhumi, 'The land of austerity.'* Interestingly, it's also known as *madhurya-dham, 'The place of divine sweetness.'* Sounds counterintuitive and contradictory. The paradox of Vrindavana, however, is that the austerity people perform here, frees them from the shackles of material entanglement and opens up a gateway to the eternal sweet reality of the spiritual world. Their future is bright and my consciousness has been illumined. A little more divine austerity may well be the order of the day. I'm slowly learning to become comfortable with the uncomfortable.

HALL OF FAME (JAN 2018)

Vrindavana is like a hall of fame. Everywhere you turn there are stories, landmarks and temples commemorating the saintly people who lived here. Ironically, they never wanted any fame. In fact, they actively avoided it – unassumingly absorbed in their daily devotion, quietly dedicating every moment of their time to forging a deep spiritual connection. They walked bare foot, meekly begged for their sustenance, bathed their minds in sacred sound and curtailed all bodily demands. They wrote prolifically, communicated truths beyond this world and compassionately made that wisdom accessible to one and all. Lives of simplicity and surrender. No envy, thoroughly honest and not a tinge of pride. Spiritual giants, no doubt.

As we tread the dusty streets of Vrindavana, we suspect there are quite a few saints walking amongst us even today. Whether we'll have the vision to detect them and whether the world will ever find out, remains to be seen. Probably not, I suspect. But it's surely comforting to know that saintly personalities of flawless calibre exist even today. Their purity generates faith and their example inspires generations. We need a living theology not just a museum of wisdom. We need to see personalities who are walking with the vision of eternity, their every movement impelled by genuine spiritual consciousness. We need individuals who are down to earth, but simultaneously in touch with transcendence, embodying everything the books talk about. The world could definitely do with a few more saints.

I often wish I could leave it all behind and live out my days in the safe company of these pure souls. Keep it simple – no more politics, no more competition, no more complexity and no more distractions. Idyllic as it sounds, I'm acutely aware that I don't possess the simplicity, absorption and sincerity to do such a thing. It can't be imitated; it has to be earned. I'll have to re-enter the complexity of the urban jungle until the hard, crushing wheel of life squeezes out the last remaining hopes of material enjoyment from my ever-curious heart. On the order of my teachers, I'll try to help a few people along the way, sharing whatever I've learnt and speaking whatever I've heard. We'll find ourselves by thinking of others. I'll try to use every bit of time and energy in a way that progresses my spiritual journey, carefully avoiding lethargy and complacency. After all is said and done, I eagerly anticipate a return to Vrindavana, hopefully with a bit more humility at my command, so I can deeply connect with the saints who eternally reside here. They know the path to eternity.

A FINAL LESSON (JAN 2018)

It's 10.30pm. I'm leaving Vrindavana in an hour, going by taxi to Delhi airport. Gathering my thoughts and making my last prayers. There's a frantic knock on the door. As I open it, a humble but insistent request shoots through: *"please let me feed you!"* It's the middle-aged South Indian devotee who stays across the courtyard. I don't know much about him, except that he always seems to be cooking; morning till evening he's covered in kitchen stains. The entire month I've overlooked him. Another face in the holy place by my material estimation. In fact, if I'm honest, my critical mind wasn't really impressed. *Why spend so much time preparing culinary delights in the transcendental land where saints curtailed their eating and instead focused on spiritual practices?* Vrindavana is the place to minimise bodily needs, I thought, and invest time in reading, chanting and praying. Take advantage of this sacred atmosphere and go deeper – cooking you can do any time. I was in for an eye-opener; one final lesson before leaving.

Unable to sidestep his fervent request, I followed him behind the courtyard, only to find a makeshift kitchen with a stack of huge pots and a feast fit for 200 people! *"It's nearly 11.00pm and everyone is sleeping!"* I said. Then he explained. Five years ago, he left behind his 'normal' life as an I.T. Specialist and relocated to Vrindavana with the sole desire to serve the residents and pilgrims of this holy place. Since then, every single day, without fail, he cooks three huge meals, goes out onto the streets and personally feeds the mendicants. *"This is the happiness of my life"* he said, *"there is nothing else of value."* He sat me down, prepared a plate, lovingly served me and then asked a favour. *"You please pray that I can carry on this service"* he pleaded. *"I want to cook more and more and feed more and more!"* During that meal, he expressed no other desire, aspiration, plan or hope for the future, other than the opportunity to feed the residents of Vrindavana for the rest of his life. Such eagerness, simplicity, purity of intent and genuine desire! This is true wealth, I thought.

It reminded me of an ancient tale. Once, while bathing, a learned sage saw a scorpion drowning. He reached forward, earnestly offering assistance, only to be violently bitten. The scorpion fell back and continued to drown. Unfazed, the sage ventured forward and did the same, only to be bitten again. An onlooker was baffled by his persistence. *"It is the scorpion's nature to bite, so I don't hold it against him"* the sage said. *"And it's my nature to serve, so I keep putting myself forward!"*

My friend, Mahesh Krishna, I'll remember that final, crucial lesson. The desire to serve others has permeated your entire being. You've internalised that spirit. It's become your nature. If that's not perfection, I don't know what is. I can't remember the last time I made a sincere

prayer, but I'll try my best as a service to you. I'll pray you continue doing what you're doing. I'll also pray to remember your example and thus remember the essence of life. Thank you for giving me my final, and ultimate, lesson in Vrindavana. Until next time.

INCREASING INTENSITY (JAN 2019)

We arrived at 2.15am in the dusty tracks of Vrindavana. It was still, calm and quiet; a timeless place, unchanged in essence, ever-exuding spiritual potency. We bowed in the dust, walked to our room and contemplated snoozing after a round-the-clock journey. At this early hour, however, Vrindavana wakes up – lights switch on, water taps begin running, bells start ringing and saintly mendicants commence their daily routine. Since we've come to capture the Vrindavana spirit, we decide to run with the local schedule. A quick bucket bath and straight out to do what everyone does before dawn.

At the temple I sat on a biting-cold marble floor, softly chanted, eyes closed and tried to tune in and focus. Calm the mind and connect with the vibration. Forget the world, disconnect and be 100% present. *Mantra* by *mantra*, chipping away the impurities. At one point I opened my eyes, happy to see the same elderly faces I have seen for years; chanting, bowing, praying and worshipping. Some things never change. On closer observation, however, I did sense a difference. Their grave demeanour indicated a measured increase in intensity. They live as lone mendicants in this holy land, probably with a vow to never leave, determined to end their days in complete spiritual absorption, diligently preparing for their imminent journey to the next world. They have understood this is the business-end of life – this is where it's make or break. Seeing them lent me my first lesson in Vrindavana – increase the intensity!

Truth be told, intensity doesn't come easily. It's actually what the champions are made of. In weight training, the level of exercise you did one year ago will no longer generate the same growth. You have to increase the repetitions, the weight or the speed of the training. One boxer said he only starts counting the push-ups *"when it starts to hurt!"* In the same way, what we did to advance our spirituality one year ago, may no longer be sufficient.

How do we step-up the intensity of our spirituality? We may want to consider increasing the *quantity* – the amount of time and effort we put in. When we think we've reached maximum capacity, we could look at increasing the *quality* – the attention and detail with which we do things. Another way is to intensify the difficulty, by accepting challenging and uncomfortable things for a higher cause. We could also increase intensity by accepting more *responsibility* and getting actively involved in empowering other people's spirituality. One way or the other, we have to *"keep the foot on the pedal."*

READ OR RELISH (JAN 2019)

I try to visit Vrindavana in an off-peak time, with no 'business,' no meetings, no responsibilities and no particular project in mind. One of my primary purposes is to engage in deep study of wisdom literature. The time, the headspace and the devotional atmosphere helps to cultivate transcendental thoughts. No excuses and no place better. It sounds wonderful and it is, but admittedly it's not always easy. I've ejected myself out of the urban mayhem, just after the busiest time of year, constantly interacting with people and with a never-ending list of tasks... and overnight I suddenly land in a quiet holy village, distanced from all the complexity, with minimal technology, all the time in the world and not a distraction in sight. It can be existentially

Relishing the Bhagavata Purana

Today I opened my books. I paused for thought. Often times I read so I can capture something exciting and inspirational to share with others. Other times I read to gain clarity and conviction, to displace doubts and deeply understand the path I walk. Sometimes I read with the hope of developing deep spiritual attraction, praying that the beautiful descriptions will flood my mind and capture my heart. Many times, I read and rest assured that it will cleanse my consciousness, even when I don't understand and I can't fully concentrate. All valid reasons and all beneficial, but all still falling short of the heart connection we seek. The reading could go deeper...

I once asked a saintly devotee how we should read. He looked somewhat surprised – *"I don't read these books"* he said, *"I relish these books!"* That moved me. It was another dimension, another relationship, another level of realisation. When he read, he was associating with God in the form of a book. There was no agenda. Transcending the mind and intellect and entering a world of unlimited spiritual possibility. I recalled how one saint's manuscript of Srimad-Bhagavatam, the anthology of pure devotion, was blotted, smudged and rendered practically unreadable due to the tears of love which were shed during his reading. We can only pray that we receive that special connection one day. Indeed, our cherished aspiration is to gain a glimpse of Sanatana Goswami's vision, who saw the Bhagavatam as his constant companion, his only friend, his source of happiness and his greatest wealth. *When, oh when?*

Truth be told, such realisations are way beyond me. Nevertheless, I'm here in Vrindavana to discover some jewels; searching, begging, praying for some invaluable insights that bring my heart into a transcendental space. A disciple once approached his Sufi teacher with a request: *"Master, I heard you've gathered many jewels from the scriptures –*

can I acquire some of them?" The master paused, reflected and finally replied: *"If I sell you those jewels you won't be able to afford them and if I give you them for free you won't appreciate them."* The disciple was disheartened. *"There is no alternative"* the master suddenly said, *"you'll have to dive into these oceanic scriptures, navigate yourself to the depths and find those priceless jewels for yourself."* The disciple understood. No shortcuts, cheap bargains or quick gains. If you want jewels, you have to mine them with effort.

MENTAL MUSCLE (JAN 2019)

Govardhana Hill is an epic place, enchanting and simultaneously educational. At every turn there is a lesson to learn. While pacing the peaceful perimeter path yesterday, a street vendor suddenly announced: *"Monkey seva! Monkey seva!"* It was an invitation to feed the mischief-making monkeys that had congregated. *"Monkey seva is my thing"* I thought, *"I've been feeding this monkey-like mind for lifetimes!"* Some nuts for our furry friends today, but the inner monkey has to diet. Walking a little further we encountered an elderly ascetic performing *'dandavat parikrama.'* After diligently bowing prostrate 108 times in the same spot, he moves forward the length of his body and repeats the process... with a vow to circumambulate the entire 25km perimeter path in that way. It's a vow that may take ten or fifteen years to complete. What focus! What dedication! What determination! I don't think my monkey-like mind could cooperate with that one.

I marvelled at the saintly mendicant's mental muscle. Most times we can't make up our mind. Even when we do, we keep changing our mind. When there are challenges, we lose our mind. The lesson is loud and clear: *"mind your mind!"* We remembered the saints of Vrindavana, who made vows which were like lines on a stone. Once they had decided they followed through, rain or shine, hell or high water. Whether life directions, spiritual commitments, or day-to-day judgements, how nice would it be if we could just make a call, have the fixity of mind to stick with it, accept the outcomes and just get on with life? I shudder to think how much time, energy and mental space we waste in constant oscillation, undecided and unsure, neither here nor there, going around in circles. Imagine we channelled all of that priceless resource in a progressive direction.

But let's face it, decisions are hard to make – after all, we have to live with them and that's scary. True, but if we don't make a call and instead decide to 'sit on the fence,' then the winds of life will inevitably appear and forcibly blow us one way or the other! Consciously decide, or unconsciously accept. It's up to us. But how do we know we are making a good decision? What is the right decision? Well, weigh it up, view it from all angles and seek advice from friends. Introspect, make a prayer and try to connect with the voice within. After all is said and done, you just have to make a call. Ultimately, the 'right' decision is the one

which is based on sober consideration, trusted consultation and true sincerity of heart. When we follow that formula, divine back up will always be there. We can't lose.

When I saw that mendicant I prayed for some mental muscle – decisiveness, confidence and fixity of mind. We have to keep moving forward and can't let the opportunities of life pass us by as we stall in the trench of procrastination, fear and indecision. We can't constantly be scared about what could go wrong, but need to start getting excited about what could go right. The quality of our decisiveness decides the quality of our life.

(N)EVER CHANGING REALITIES (OCT 2022)

I deliberately select extra-long stopovers for connecting flights. It's an idiosyncrasy that drives my travel partners up the wall! Aside from the satisfaction of saving a few pennies, I find my time at airports to be extremely rewarding. They are like full-stops in the narrative of life. Just as the punctuation mark closes one thought and allows the beginning of another, airport transit lounges represent the conclusion of one adventure and the commencement of another. Thus, 'airport-time' gives me 'reflection time'; naturally inspiring me to look back and reflect, look forward and realign, and peacefully sit in the present, grateful for it all. Learning from the past, planning for the future and all the while appreciating the present – the art of life! What can I say, international airport lounges have become my second home.

Today is an eight-hour stopover at Frankfurt International, reflecting on an eventful few months. It feels like life has shifted a gear in formality, responsibility and overall intensity. Yet it's a great opportunity. With a new role in the community comes the necessity to redefine my individuality, but also find a deep authenticity so there can be sustainability. It's a small attempt to continue venturing beyond the safety that breeds mediocrity. If I have the genuine sincerity and humility, then it will surely awaken a higher quality of spirituality. (This post has inadvertently morphed into poetry... it must be destiny!)

But I don't think I'm alone – everyone's life changes – our health changes, fortunes change, careers change, the people surrounding us change, world situations change. We're living in an ever-changing world, a virtual reality of transient conditions.

Amidst the ever-changing reality, however, is the never-changing reality. In a few hours I'll catch a flight to Delhi, enroute to the holy town of Vrindavana. Thousands of pilgrims will descend here in the coming month for spiritual rejuvenation. I'm anticipating the smell of cow-dung fires, the unbroken ringing of temple gongs, ascetics around every corner and the natural, heartfelt devotion that envelopes everything. In Vrindavana, we go beyond the ever-changing identities, abilities and facilities that we define and value ourselves by. In Vrindavana, popularity, position and productivity fades into insignificance. In Vrindavana, we enter as beggars, desperately seeking divine communion. In Vrindavana, we remember that although everything changes, in reality nothing changes.

At birth, I received the name '*Sandeep.*' When I became a novice monk, they called me '*Bhakta Sandeep.*' Later on, I was ordained with the name '*Sutapa Das.*' Nowadays, they call me a '*Swami.*' Behind all those names is a beggar, trying to connect with the never-changing reality that somehow feels much more accessible in the power packed Vrindavan village. May I glimpse the real Vrindavana, where, since every moment is spent in selfless loving service, there is no past or future, but simply the eternal present. That is the real reality.

THE CITY THAT NEVER SLEEPS (OCT 2022)

This evening I'm at the Radha Damodara temple. Neither large nor ornate, hidden away in an obscure gully of Vrindavana, the unassuming entrance gives no hint of what's inside. It's an Aladdin's cave! The penetrating vibrations from centuries of singing, spiritual discourse and heartfelt prayer by saints of the highest calibre pulsates through the ether. The atmosphere is amplified by the overflowing pilgrims eagerly seeking divine grace. This is where it all comes alive. This is living theology. While being squashed I scan the crowd and realise I have lots to learn – the renunciation of the ascetics, the simple devotion of the white-saree widows, the innocence of the playful children and the spiritual greed of the eager pilgrims. Who knows who they all are? They're all awake to the spiritual reality. Vrindavana is truly the city that never sleeps, early mornings to late evenings, tireless devotees entering the timeless world.

There's a correlation. When we snap out of spiritual slumber, we simultaneously begin to lose interest in sleep. Even Krishna is renowned for staying awake all night in Vrindavana! The ascetic saints of yore reduced their resting to one or two hours a day – and sometimes they overlooked even that. How can you forget to sleep? Is it humanly possible? I don't think so – clearly, they were accessing superhuman states due to profound spiritual absorption. When reality is better than dreams, there is no impetus to switch off. One writer says that dreams are not what happen when you go to sleep, dreams are what prevent you from going to sleep!

So what does it mean for us? We can first ask whether we see sleep as a duty or a drug. Someone once said to me *"sleep is my drug, the bed is my dealer and the alarm clock is the police!"* How we dread the first wakeup call of the day! In progressive life, however, we don't live to sleep, but rather we sleep to live. Krishna says you can't be a yogi if you sleep too much or sleep too little. Prabhupada added, *"if you sleep too much you become lazy, if you sleep too little you become crazy."* We need sleep and we all need a different amount. But remember, sleep is not an end in itself.

Observing our sleep patterns can be revealing. Part of our sleep is to replenish the physical body, a percentage to recharge the cognitive functions and then there is a portion to deal with our emotional state. When we're attacked by boredom, lack of direction, frustration, anxiety or insecurity, we tend to slip towards oversleeping. Fighting with alarm clocks is a likely sign that life is still not in the right place. If doing nothing (i.e., sleeping) is more inspiring than doing something, it means whatever we're doing is not inspiring enough. Purpose is the best alarm clock in the world – that reverberating chime in the heart is the real wake up call. May Vrindavana, the city that never sleeps, amplify my purpose and keep me awake with not a moment to waste.

DOG FIGHTS (OCT 2022)

You have to be careful what you write about, especially in Vrindavana. Last week I discussed *'The City that Never Sleeps'* and yesterday I found myself awake for most of the night – all because of barking dogs! Of the external disturbances in Vrindavana, dog fights are around the clock. Even vehicle horns trail off at a certain hour, but not our canine friends. They're relentless. One confronts another, growling and howling, and before you know it there's a crowd, fierce dispute, barking and commotion, all about nothing. After all is settled, it just needs another petty trigger and everything is ignited again. Like this, all night long.

Awake in bed, I couldn't help but think how many 'dog fights' I've had in my own life. Needless arguments, petty squabbles, energy-sapping friction and conflict over nothing that significant. I am a self-confessed victim of the 'Age of Quarrel.' Barking and howling, getting all worked up about relatively minor things – from road rage to family feuds, people's idiosyncrasies to miscommunication, perceptions of situations to feelings of injustice. Of course, there are times when we have to stand up for what's right. We can't just ignore everything that needs rectification. My sense, however, is that for most of us, nine out of ten disputes are uncalled for. Either they're unimportant in the bigger picture or resolvable through other means. No need to fight, because even when we win an argument, generally we lose – we lose relationships, we lose perspective, we lose peace of mind, we lose focus, we lose energy. The winner is often the biggest loser.

Yesterday was a wake-up call (though I never really fell asleep in the first place!). I can't afford to waste time in unnecessary friction and conflict. Every disagreement doesn't have to be an argument. When we mediate the relationships of this world nicely, we open up the opportunity to meditate on matters of eternal significance. Thank you, Vrindavana, for reminding me not to lose any sleep over useless dog fights. Maybe if we quieten that noisy commotion, we'll instead hear the enchanting and mystical vibration that pervades this spiritual land – the divine flute song that captures the mind, enlivens the consciousness and conquers the heart. We have the choice over what will reverberate in our hearts and minds – the injustices of this world, or the grace and beauty of the other world.

THE FESTIVAL OF MAGIC (OCT 2022)

On Diwali, the festival of lights, as we celebrate the demise of the 10-headed demon Ravana, I refocus on removing 10 mindsets that overshadow my life and block real happiness:

1. The lust which breeds self-centredness

2. The greed to be better than others

3. The pride which stops us from improving

4. The illusion of pretending to be someone else

5. The anger of over-reacting to petty things

6. The envy in seeing someone else's success

7. The ambition that breeds immoral acts

8. The harshness of jumping to conclusions

9. The madness of not learning from mistakes

10. The insecurity of losing temporary things

More than a cultural festival, Diwali is meant to be magically transformational.

LOVE OVER FEAR (NOV 2022)

Fear and love are perhaps the two most powerful emotions in creation. Fear is the inbuilt warning system to avoid all pain, and love is the sweet call which invites the heart to melt. Of the two, love reigns supreme. When we have love, all fear disappears and Vrindavana, the abode of love, is the living proof. Ancient stories tell of Krishna's parents, who, driven by love, followed Krishna's daring call to abandon cultural and generational traditions of ritual worship to the heavenly God and instead embrace a higher-level spirituality. Their love for Him outweighed the fear (and eventual reality) of supernatural backlash. Krishna's friends fearlessly frolicked with destructive demons, powerful and brutal, knowing His loving eyes were right behind them. When Krishna's girlfriends heard His flute call, they impulsively ran to meet Him in the dead of night, with no inhibitions of violating custom, jeopardising physical safety, facing social repercussion or damaging future security. The fears which define and drive most people's lives disappeared in their oceanic love.

This phenomenon continues today. In Vrindavana you encounter individuals who have embarked on life trajectories that the calculative mind just can't grasp. They've taken risks, made sacrifices, embraced uncertainty and let go of things that most people wouldn't dream of. There's no rational explanation to decode why they do what they do – it's a deep, invisible, heartfelt conviction impelling them forward. The lesson is loud and clear: real life begins when we find an object of love that so comprehensively consumes our consciousness that fear has no place left to reside.

When we're impoverished in love, or directing that love toward the wrong object, fear dominates – fears about the future, fears about relationships, fears about the world, fears about health, fears of rejection. In happy times we fear it will end, in distress we fear it may never end! Our life decisions usually reflect our fears more than our dreams, our thinking process haunted by what may go wrong. People accuse religion of being driven by fear, but practically everyone is driven by fear. In reality, it's only deep, heartfelt, divine connection that can catapult you beyond fear.

In Vrindavana, there is no God and there is no fear-driven religion. Here we encounter Krishna, who isn't simply a Lord to be fearful of, or the father to be dutiful towards, but the most charming personality in creation – one who may just steal all your attention! Here people have heart attacks, not just physical, but spiritual ones too. Krishna mystically appears. If you're lucky enough to lose your heart in Vrindavana, you'll witness all your fears disappear at the same time. *When, oh when?*

Today I ask myself: *when all is said and done, will my life be defined by love or fear?*

TRANSFORMING INTO YOURSELF (NOV 2022)

They say you never return from Vrindavana the same person. The spiritual impressions created here run deep, transforming the heart and mind in mysterious ways. It's also clear that we don't enter Vrindavana as the same person. Compared to previous visits, you can detect the change in perception, receptivity, absorption and focus. Whether the short and powerful spiritual injection of a sacred

A joyful resident of Vrindavan

pilgrimage, or the sustained and dedicated day-to-day practices in our home base, both have their unique transformational effects. When consciousness transforms, it opens the doors to unchartered spiritual territory – not because we gain access to something new, but because we begin penetrating deeper into the same truths. The scholar-saints define the Supreme Spirit and the ancient literatures as *purana*, which literally means 'the oldest.' They say *purana* can also mean *nava pura,* or 'filled with freshness.' As we transform into our pure self, the 'oldest' is experienced in 'ever-fresh' ways!

Transformation is fascinating. Whether it's a blossoming plant producing fruits, simple ingredients morphing into a culinary delight, or a baby maturing into a unique grown-up. For me, however, witnessing the inner transformation from spiritual practice is most fascinating. It makes the path exciting, hope-giving and tangible. It makes everything real! Transformation takes us from ritual to experience, from following rules to finding reality. Transformation turns religion into spirituality. Transformation is crucial for our own faith, because without it, we begin to doubt the value of our path. Transformation is the most powerful proof of spirituality. When someone challenged Bhaktivedanta Swami, thinking him one of India's mystical god-men, about what miracle he could perform, the Swami pointed at his disciples and said *"they are my miracle!"* When a person's faith, character, desires, aspirations and entire vision of life can transform, it proves the unparalleled power of spirituality.

But what if we don't feel like we're transforming? Well, consider, in the proportionately limited time we've given to spirituality, how much has changed. On estimate, we may only have given 5% of the effort and endeavour we invest in worldly pursuits. Think about the time, energy and sacrifice people put into academic endeavours, bringing up a family, developing a career or securing a living space. People spend years on such things, losing track of time. Practically everyone, without exception, spends 15 years of life, 5 days a week, for a 'material' education. Imagine if everyone dedicated 1.5 years of life (10% of that) for spiritual education. People are willing to turn their life upside-down to cash-in on a career prospect, but who would make similar sacrifices to avail of spiritual opportunities? If small investments have generated significant change, logic tells us significant investments will trigger massive transformation. What we put in, is what we'll get out. Thank you, Vrindavana, for reminding me of the most pressing question: *what did I invest into my eternal transformation today?*

FROZEN IN ETERNITY (NOV 2022)

It's time to head back. I could miss the flight, lose my passport and slip right back into Vrindavana life... chappatis and dahl, wandering the sacred tracks, immersing in scripture, singing into the early hours. We could adopt the determination of the ascetics and old widows, leaving Vrindavana only when the ashes from the funeral pyre merge into the River Yamuna and float downstream. Realistic? Probably not. The holy month concludes and pilgrims disperse, the temperature drops as winter looms and another year in the material world gradually winds up. Vrindavana, however, remains forever unchanged, steeped in a devotional time-warp. The singing goes on, the bells, cymbals and drums steadily reverberate and offerings at the rustic shrines, saturated with raw, unpolished affection, continue. Vrindavana's devotional fervour perpetuates, day after day, as it has for generations. When you return, nothing's changed. Old is gold – timeless transcendental tradition. Those who reside here in spirit, live in the eternal present, oblivious to the ever-changing tides and trends of the so-called 'real' world, deeply content with simple devotion in the here and now.

How beautiful to live in the eternal present! I reflect on my own life which, for the most part, is out of sync. Eagerly planning the future, regularly drifting to the past, but seldom relishing complete presence in the present. The self-development gurus highlight the 'Power of Now,' urging us to check the overthinking mind from hijacking the opportunity to fully experience life. A good proposition, but not so easy. The Bhagavad-gita reveals that it's not a psychological adjustment, tip, trick or technique that roots you in the present. That will never sustain. What we really need is deep spiritual connection with the identity, life and activities we've assumed. The real reason we glide to the past or chronically fast forward to the future, is because the present hasn't captured our imagination. It's just not exciting or enthralling enough. The present is an anti-climax and thus we restlessly gravitate to the past or future.

Time plays out in different ways. There is *clock time*, consisting of the seconds, minutes and hours which govern our day. Then there is *biological time* - our body clock which intuitively operates according to its unique cyclical pattern. There is also *psychological time*, or the relative experience of time according to our emotional state - we've seen how time flies when you're having fun. The spiritual dimension, however, rests in *timelessness* - the 'eternal present' - a space of consciousness in which we transcend every conception of time. In Vrindavana we encounter an existence free from ethereal past or future. Though Vrindavana is undoubtedly a transcendent abode and earthly pilgrimage site, it's ultimately a mysterious space of consciousness. This magical space is actually the simplest and most accessible of all experiences. To access it, the aspirant must uncover their innermost authentic spiritual persona, craft a life in which everything connects to it and then fully embrace the opportunity to live it out. At that time, we 'drop time' and effortlessly rest in the eternal present. Life's roles and responsibilities go on, but our consciousness is in another dimension. This is the only way to experience the Power of Now.

Thank you Vrindavana, for renewing my desire to rediscover the eternal present. May I one day discover that life, in which I become frozen in eternity.

For some people, questioning comes easy. Their natural inquisitiveness, sensitivity and ability to process information means they can quickly pose a penetrating inquiry. It's an art worth learning. Through deeper probing we're able to contextualise wisdom, unearth hidden jewels of insight and decode how to apply and incorporate it in our own lives. In dialogue we have the opportunity to express doubts, confusions and opinions and simultaneously address the human story behind the spiritual ideals. Powerful questions are like a master key, opening us to a world of living wisdom. Thus, especially in spiritual circles, the question-answer format is perpetually utilised.

In this section, we try to address the different questions that people have asked over the years. Some deal with the life of a monk, others with relationships, community and how to navigate the complexities of life. We delve into philosophy and theology, contrasting that with science and spirituality and dissecting the interaction between them. In these exchanges, the knowledge comes to life and we begin to access layers of understanding which were previously hidden.

ASK A
MONK

Questions & Answers

MONK'S LIFE

When you hear the word 'monk' it could trigger stereotyped images in your mind; a lonely path between you and God, characterised by introspection and solitude, seriousness and gravity, silence and sameness, involving self-denial and strictness in all aspects of life. In many traditions monasticism is tantamount to social death, a path walked by a small minority. In the Hare Krishna tradition, monasticism has its own unique flavour. I'll try to depict that for you, drawing on my experiences as a monk over the last two decades.

Speaking about myself is always challenging because I'm really just a 'work-in-progress,' neither special nor outstanding by any stretch of the imagination. Here, however, I share some reflections, hoping that the human story of a soul trying to fly in the skies of spirituality awakens something within you. The goal of life is not simply to break free from all bonds, but to then become completely conquered in divine love. For some individuals, living as a monk for either a significant period, or the entirety of their life, can be the most rewarding and suitable life-path. For others, the principles of monasticism can still be employed and applied in whatever situation they find themselves in.

What attracted you to monastic life?

A foundational teaching of the Bhagavad-gita is that this life is one chapter in a much longer story. There was a history before and what we experience here is preparing us for a journey beyond. According to our previous lives, the activities and desires we cultivated, we enter this world with a particular *svabhava* (psychophysical disposition) and a stock of *karma* (destined consequences). It's a fascinating insight and helps us understand the varieties and personalities we see in the world. Some of us are outgoing, while others are grave. Some are studious and critically minded, whereas others are simpler and more straightforward. Some of us naturally tune into spirituality, whereas others find it uninteresting and irrelevant.

Thus, I guess my attraction to monastic life is likely rooted in previous lives, though I don't know the exact details. One thing I detected very early on in life was my inclination towards simplicity, minimalism and solitude. I was averse to accumulation and it actually became stressful to wear expensive clothes or have extra things above what I really needed. The idea of making money felt more like a burden than something exciting. To be honest, even wearing a suit and tie was an ordeal! Most of what I saw people running after - titles, achievements, status symbols and security - seemed unnecessary. It didn't resonate with me.

I didn't, however, really have any spiritual teachings behind it - these were just feelings and thoughts. Naturally I was a little confused about what I'd do in life because the typical goals that the world sets were not moving my heart, yet I couldn't really identify an alternative. When I contacted the teachings of the Bhagavad-gita, however, it began to explain the feelings that sat deep within me. Furthermore, when I learned about the path of renunciation, it gave me a vision of how to live out those inclinations towards simplicity. So from day one, the monks were fascinating to me. Hearing of saints and sages who turned away from the world and lived with nothing spoke to my heart and captured my imagination. I guess I was being drawn towards my *dharma* – my calling and purpose – what I was wired for.

How were you introduced to the teachings?

In my family the Bhagavad-gita was a known but unknown book. It was present as a familiar name, but nobody had ever really read it. When I was fifteen, a curiosity sprouted in my heart to find out more about spirituality, life and what more there may be beyond the nine to five. To this day I'm not sure what triggered it. Life was good, no major issues or problems, a pretty smooth ride, yet it felt like something was missing.

One day I went to the library and borrowed several translations of the Bhagavad-gita, but I couldn't really get anything from them. They were too complex, too abstract and too poetically fuzzy! Some weeks later, one of my school friends said a Hare Krishna had knocked at his door and left a Bhagavad-gita (As It Is). I took it as a sign, asked him if I could borrow it and walked home with it the very next day. I sat in my room anticipating what I would learn as I opened this treasure house. I was full of excitement and anticipation. After one page, however, I closed it shut! Too complex – the language, the concepts, the philosophy! But this time the experience had some substance to it. On one hand I didn't understand anything, but on the other hand I felt this deep intuition that I was holding something extremely profound.

So, I tried reading again, slower, bit by bit. I started grasping some of the ideas and was trying to piece it all together. These were the days before the internet, before Google and Wikipedia, so there was no go-to place to simplify it. No shortcuts - you had to sit down and figure it out by yourself! So, that's what I was trying to do. The real gamechanger was when I started coming to the temple and asking the monks questions. In a single conversation with them I would learn more than the months of reading I did alone. They had a knack to make it clear and bring it alive. In those meetings with the monks, I felt as though I could just sit there for hours hearing them explain this philosophy and its relevance to life.

What was your experience of university life?

By eighteen I had already been meditating, chanting, reading and befriending Krishna devotees for a few years. Spirituality had become my passion and biggest interest in life. I got good A-Level grades and was preparing for university. One of my main considerations was to go somewhere and study something that would help me develop my spirituality. I wanted to study Philosophy or Theology but was convinced to do something which would get me a proper job! In the end I opted to study BSc Information Management at University College London (UCL).

My university years were extremely revealing. I was navigating a parallel existence, contrasting the material and spiritual. My university accommodation was five minutes from the Central London Hare Krishna Temple. On one night I'd be out doing what university students do best and the very next morning I'd be at the temple. I was juxtaposing two lives – I witnessed both approaches and started seeing the futility of one and the unassuming beauty of the other. It was a life-changing time, and also quite scary. I started sensing that my life path was going in a very different direction to 99% of the people around me.

We also had a Krishna Consciousness Society at UCL which began to take over my life. Now I wasn't just learning spirituality, but actively sharing it with others. We were organising events, creating promotional material, trying to reach the masses with a provoking spiritual message and, in the process, discussing, debating and interfacing with all kinds of people. It was an incredible adventure and really deepened my commitment and conviction. For the first time in my life, I was 'on a mission' and had some real purpose. You could say I became a spiritual activist!

When did you decide to become a monk?

I was nearing graduation and naturally thinking about my future. As mentioned before, the aspirations and goals that most of my fellow course mates had didn't really excite me. In fact, I remember going for an interview in Holborn for a graduate position. As I was in the reception area waiting to be called, I looked around at the open office and everyone in that corporate environment – it was so existentially unnerving that I just decided to walk out before the person even called me! That was perhaps my first and last interview in the corporate world and technically it didn't even happen!

But I had to do *something* with my life. An idea and opportunity to travel to India for six months came up. It ticked all the boxes. India was the land of spirituality; it would allow me to disconnect from London and all the voices of expectations. I was inspired by the amazing ashrams and holy places I could visit. There was, however, one complexity – convincing my family. Naturally they expected me to go straight into work, do well in my career, eventually get married, start a family and go on to lead a successful 'normal' life. You can't blame them, it's the cherished dream of practically every parent. So this period became perhaps the most testing and emotional of my entire life thus far.

I had to choose between comfort and aspiration – tread the path of least resistance or journey into the unknown. I had to decide whether to accept the discomfort of going against the grain, or potentially face the depression of regret. Heated discussions and emotional exchanges became a daily affair. I often thought of just ditching the idea, getting a job and keeping everyone happy. But then my heart would tell me – *"you've come this close; you can't give up now."* Now I look back, I realised I had to go through that to really deepen my conviction and clarify why I was doing this. The struggle of that period helped me develop an inner resolve and determination to walk my path. It built a real seriousness within me. As a kid, I had never really gone against my family, but this time there was no other choice. I knew I had to do this.

So when I was twenty-one, I went to India. I met amazing people, visited amazing places, did amazing things and had the most amazing experiences. The beauty and simplicity of monastic life captured me. I slowly began to see the pieces of the puzzle coming together – my desire to deepen my spirituality, the natural inclination towards simplicity and minimalism, finding a meaningful contribution to make in the world. Becoming a monk seemed to incorporate and integrate everything seamlessly. Internally I knew I had to pursue monastic life, but after six months away I landed back in London and had to muster up more courage to take the next step.

How did you make the decision to live at Bhaktivedanta Manor?

Bhaktivedanta Manor Hare Krishna Temple, the UK headquarters of the movement, is a place I regularly visited since I was born. My parents brought me here for cultural festivals and Sunday worship and

From 2002 - 2022

there were always strong memories of it. When I returned from India, I concluded it was the place to continue my journey. I didn't want to make any big decisions, but instead told my family I'd be living here for another year to deepen my spiritual roots and consolidate what I'd learnt in India. Naturally they were unhappy and most of all, scared. They sensed this was becoming more than a temporary infatuation. I soldiered on and braved the storm, determined that I wouldn't look back in my life with regrets. One monk told me *"it's better to have loved and lost than never to have loved at all!"* It was ironic that he used that line to describe my journey into celibate renunciation, but it did make sense. I had to give this a try, even if in the end it didn't work out.

So, I became a monk at the Manor, and began doing everything that the junior monks do – study, cook, clean, engage in missionary activities, shadow the seniors, learn instruments etc. I felt as though I had graduated from material university and was now entering spiritual university. It required an adjustment. Living communally with people from such diverse backgrounds, following a highly regulated and monitored regime, and having minimal contact with material society and activities, were all big changes. Naturally there were days when I questioned my decision. On most days, however, I found myself in flow state, feeling totally at home.

One year turned into two, before I knew it two turned into five and then I passed the decade mark and realised this really was my calling. Over 20 years later I continue to live as a monk and feel like I'm still learning just like on day one of entering the monastery.

How do monks engage with the modern world?

There are different types of monks. I guess the first type is the 'reclusive monk.' That's the one that most imagine in their mind – the one that retreats into a cave, disappears into the forest, or climbs to the top of a mountain, going deeper within and moving away from the external world. Those kinds of monks become socially dead and embrace complete solitude and seclusion. If I'm honest, that life was actually quite attractive to me because by nature I'm introverted and shy, and so I had the hope that monastic life would give me this experience.

There is, however, another type of monk called an 'engaged monk.' These monastics live within their own sacred space, but then reach out and engage with society. They seek to help the mass of people in society and make spirituality relevant and practical for those in the 'real world.' Sometimes we call them urban monks, or modern monks. You'll find them in high streets, city centres, universities, corporate firms, in people's living rooms, teaching and sharing spiritual knowledge. Though they live a life of renunciation, their main focus is service and missionary work.

Although I was introverted by nature, I also had this desire to help others. Being an engaged monk helped me honour both aspects. From day one, although I feared public speaking, it was something I was practically forced to do. Every speaking engagement carried a mixed experience – a nervousness, discomfort and unease with being in the spotlight, but then an incredible sense of satisfaction, joy and growth after doing it, knowing that I had shared something invaluable that could change people's lives. In this way, sharing wisdom and communicating with the world became my day job and I've never stopped doing that. Over twenty years later, hardly a day goes by where I'm not addressing an audience in some forum, trying to share wisdom in relevant, dynamic and transformational ways. I thought monastic life would offer predictability and sameness, but nowadays I'm not sure what country I'll be in next week. It's interesting how life turns out!

What convinced you to enter life-long renunciation?

Once you reach your forties you naturally begin thinking about your long-term future. My spiritual teacher and other prominent mentors observed me over the years and felt there was an opportunity for me to take a further step and increase my responsibility. For twenty years I had been a living as a *brahmacari*, or a student monk. Generally, once *brahmacaris* complete their training they get married, start a family and begin a career in the world. That is a beautiful path and many of my good friends have gone on to do wonderful things after graduating from monastic life. Some *brahmacaris*, however, decide to embrace life-long renunciation in which they symbolically 'close all the doors' and dedicate their entire life to monasticism and celibacy. This is known as *sannyasa*, or the 'final vow.' It is said that the *sannyasi* gives up the relatively small world of family life, to embrace the whole world as his family. *Sannyasa* is about marrying the mission of spiritual welfare work, investing the totality of one's mind, words and actions in spiritual activity.

After deep contemplation, soul-searching, prayer and heartfelt conversation with my guides, I decided to embrace life-long renunciation. It was a big step and involved five years of preparation. On Sunday 26th June 2022 I took the vows of lifetime renunciation and my name was changed from 'Sutapa Das' to 'Svayam Bhagavan Keshava Swami' (or 'Keshava Swami' for short).

It's strange, because when you take *sannyasa* it's almost as though everything changes but nothing changes! When you wake up the next morning there is formality, respect, responsibility and social expectations. Everything becomes bigger, more public, and people interact with you differently. You carry the renunciate's staff with you and naturally stand out from the crowd. It dawns on you that life will

never be the same again. In another sense, however, nothing changes – you study the same books and continue the same spiritual program. You realise that all the inner imperfections have not magically disappeared and you have to keep working on yourself. It would be the greatest illusion to think you've become an overnight success. For me *sannyasa* was not an achievement, but rather an opportunity to journey into a deeper experience of transcendence.

RELATIONSHIPS

Though I'm able to comfortably engage with people, my personality type veers more towards the introvert and thus I never actively invested in bonding with people on a deeper level. That's why monasticism seemed like a good fit. Ironically, after becoming a monk, I realised this was one of my major shortcomings. The support, friendship, encouragement and faith that we receive in loving, spiritual relationships, helps us rise to newer heights in the spiritual sky. In the company of inspired spiritualists, you can make quantum leaps.

That said, navigating relationships in this world, is not always easy. Firstly, not all relationships are inherently spiritual – what about friends and family who don't follow your path, colleagues who you rub shoulders with everyday and dependents who you can't control or force? Then there are complexities within spiritual friendships, which are not always as smooth and amicable as we would imagine. Though we share the same philosophy we may still clash on personality. Learning how to interact, relate and connect with others is amongst the most important of life skills.

How do we manage the expectations of others?

Once, the disagreement between a married couple became so acute that they had to settle it in court. There, they began arguing in front of the judge! The wife demanded, *"I want my son to become an accountant!"* while the husband countered, *"I want him to become a doctor!"* As it went back and forth, each side stubbornly defending their corner, the judge interjected and innocently asked, *"Why don't you just ask your son what he wants to be?"* The couple looked at the judge incredulously – *"our son is not even born yet!"*

It's scary how much expectation lands on our shoulders from family and friends. On top of it all is the added pressure from society, media and the general trends of the world. How do we manage it all?

We must acknowledge that everyone's expectations don't hold equal weight. If you try to please everyone in life, you'll end up pleasing no one. So, whose expectations should we take seriously? Well, if someone knows you well, your strengths, weaknesses, your hopes and dreams, the history of your journey, then naturally their expectations count for more. In sanskrit we say they are sajatiya, or likeminded. In addition, if they love you, genuinely want you to be the best you can, and are a sincere well-wisher, then they are empowered not just by head, but by heart. This is known as snigdha, or natural feelings of affection. Further, if they are spiritually wise, mature, experienced and equipped with deeper vision, then their insights can take you far. This is known as asraya, or the spiritual qualification to give shelter and help.

In essence, while you can draw something from everyone, the expectations of those who know you (sajatiya), love you (snigdha) and can genuinely help you (asraya), count for more.

Should we befriend people who have different opinions?

Once I saw a billboard which read – *"Every disagreement doesn't have to be an argument."* It made a lot of sense. It's not that friends can't have different opinions. It's not that friends can't have different likes. It's not that friends can't have different ways of looking at the world and approaching life. It's that variety which actually enriches our existence. Variety is the mother of enjoyment!

If we respond to disagreements in an appropriate way, with respect, patience and genuine desire to understand, it can actually elevate our consciousness. It's not that the truth is always black and white. They say I have my version of the truth, you have your version of the truth and then there's the real truth! The problem is that we think, I'm right, they're wrong, or they're right, I'm wrong. But perhaps we are both right to an extent and then there's a higher right, probably beyond what both of us can grasp at this moment in time. Maybe they have a piece of the truth that I'm missing and maybe I have a piece of the truth that they're missing.

So yes, I think part of progressive life is to wrestle (in a healthy way) with opposing opinions. Just as resistance builds muscle, engaging with opposing opinions nurtures your thinking. Talk to people who have a different take on life. Don't enter the discourse simply to 'win' or have your voice heard, instead allow the questions, doubts and opinions of others genuinely challenge and clarify your own understanding.

How do we forgive someone who has hurt us?

The goal of life is not to remember all the terrible things that someone has done to you, but rather to remember all the wonderful, divine things that are happening to you every single day. But while we're hijacked by these negative thoughts, emotions and bitterness towards others, we don't have the headspace to fully acknowledge the beauty in our lives. Forgiveness is essential because it frees up room in our consciousness. The spiritual knowledge of the Bhagavad-gita gives three essential insights which help us to forgive.

Firstly, we develop a deeper vision of ourselves. We are spirit souls on a journey through different chapters of life and all of our current experiences are connected to previous acts. This is a not a chapter of life which is in isolation. So, when someone sends some negativity towards us, when someone seemingly does something unreasonable, illogical, impulsive and hurtful, we know there is a higher reason why we're going through this. It helps us avoid imprisoning ourselves into victim mentality. Other people are the messengers of our *karma*, delivering us lessons that we need to learn. Rather than holding them responsible for my difficulties, I instead take that responsibility myself.

Another insight that facilitates forgiveness is when we have the humility and honesty to realise we also made many mistakes. We have been unkind to others. We've also fallen prey to the human weaknesses of anger, greed, envy, pride or harshness. Thus, we appreciate that people are weak. We can't be judges for other people's mistakes and then lawyers for our own. There will be times when we will make mistakes and we'll require the broadmindedness of others to forgive us.

Finally, forgiveness becomes easier when we appreciate that the world is meant to be uncomfortable and frustrating. The world is meant to be imperfect, but the Bhagavad-gita explains it's 'perfectly imperfect.' In other words, all the problems and discomfort of this world are meant to remind us that we're not made for this realm. We can thus forgive, because we can appreciate that whatever we went through is ultimately an impetus moving us towards eternal freedom.

Forgiveness, empowered by these deep insights, becomes much more possible. The greatest personalities in our tradition were able to forgive even the greatest injustices, because they were empowered with this broad vision of reality.

Wouldn't the notion that *"I deserved this injustice"* be harmful on an individual and societal level?

To realise that others are the 'messengers of our karma' doesn't mean we're saying:

1) The wrong that other people do is ok

2) That we shouldn't take practical action to defend / protect ourselves

3) That we are bad people and 'deserve it'

Rather, a progressive spiritualist will ensure that those who cause pain to others are corrected and reformed. Further, they surely make practical arrangements for their self-care and protection.

Along with this practical response, however, the spiritualist has a deeper mindset. When we rise beyond the simplistic notion that the pain of this world is random and indiscriminate, we actually hold the key to pacifying the heart on the deepest level. Every event, experience and emotion provides deep insight into the nature of the world, the self and the deeper purpose of life. Nobody deserves to suffer – the law of *karma* is not about pointing fingers, but a complex and intriguing facet of nature that aids us in the journey towards deeper spiritual discovery. *Karma* should never be insensitively used to judge others, but compassionately employed in our own personal introspection. If spiritual wisdom doesn't leave you feeling more empowered, hopeful and hungry for life, there is a good chance it has been misrepresented, misapplied or miscommunicated.

How do we respond to the faults we see in committed spiritual practitioners?

One thing I've learnt in my spiritual journey is that years in a spiritual movement is not the sole measure of spiritual maturity. That doesn't mean we shouldn't respect those who have been practicing for many years, but in reality, it's not the number of years in your life, it's the amount of life in those years. So, we shouldn't have an unrealistic or utopian vision of spiritual practitioners.

When we do detect some 'fault,' the first thing would be to acknowledge that we could well be wrong. Furthermore, when we see faults in others and discrepancies around us, it's often a reflection of something within ourselves. If something is agitating me, attracting my attention and disturbing me so much, it may mean that some elements of those things are within me as well. Do I sometimes fall prey to that weakness? The great teacher, Bhaktisiddhanta Saraswati Thakur, said *"When faults in others misguide you, then be patient, introspect and look for faults within yourself. Know that nobody can harm you unless you harm yourself."*

Secondly, spiritual vision means to not just see how far someone is from the ideal, but to appreciate also how far they have progressed and improved from where they were. If someone is progressing, if they are proverbially 'in the shower' and cleansing their consciousness, it would be unreasonable to write them off for being unclean.

Thirdly, faults in others should not decrease your faith in the power of the spiritual tradition. I can share with you innumerable stories of accomplished people I have spent time with. I used to think saints were people of the past, the personalities we read about in scriptures, but then I started witnessing saints walk in front of me. One type of person sceptically looks around, picks up on bad examples and concludes that's the standard. Alternatively, we can look around with a gracious heart and see amazing examples and be inspired by that. Let us not descend to the lowest common denominator but rather look at those who are flying high in the spiritual sky.

How does the Bhagavad-gita help you cope with the loss of a loved one?

The Bhagavad-gita begins by giving us philosophical insight. Krishna explains that there is no such thing as death. When someone 'passes away' it's not a full stop, but just a comma – a gateway to the next chapter of life. Krishna equips us with a broader vision which gives perspective to the natural shock and loss that we feel.

Secondly, Krishna teaches us how to be emotionally sensitive. Some days after Arjuna heard the whole philosophy of the Gita, his son, Abhimanyu, died on the battlefield. Arjuna went to that spot and seeing his son, there was a natural outpour of paternal affection. Krishna supported him through his process of grieving. Soon after, Arjuna picked up his bow and continued fighting.

This is very instructive. Even though Arjuna was fully equipped with spiritual knowledge, there was still a natural process of grieving. It is completely normal to feel pain when losing the company of a loved one. The pain is like a wound which requires attention and ultimately takes time to heal. When someone is grieving, they are not always in the right state of mind to hear philosophy. First, we give them friendship, comfort and help in practical ways. Then when the emotions settle, combined with loving friendship, philosophical discussion goes deeper. When we lose someone we realise life will never be the same, but life can still be beautiful.

The Gita also teaches us that someone leaving this world is a golden opportunity to reflect more deeply on the temporality and transience of our own lives. It's an alarm clock, meant to wake us up to higher priorities. These are moments which inspire us to upgrade the way in which we spend our valuable time and energy.

Why do we need spiritual company?

A famous saying tells us, *"If you're the smartest person in the room, you need to change room."* We need to surround ourselves with people who challenge us to learn more, dream more, do more, become more, achieve more and discover more! Thus, being around sincere spiritual practitioners is so powerful. Not just because we are all 'in the club' and it's some kind of social clique. Rather, it's more to do with the dynamic energy, encouragement and excitement that you generate in that company. Everyone is learning and growing, and everyone else is feeding off that and benefitting from it.

If we surround ourselves with materialistic people, it will be difficult to break out of the box and all the invisible boundaries that the world has imprisoned us within. The biggest lie in the world is that material arrangements, achievements and facilities will make us happy. It takes a lot to go beyond that conception and really live with a different vision.

When we're encouraged to associate with spiritual people, it's not about creating an elitist club or looking down on others. Rather, we want to surround ourselves with people who are going to positively challenge and uplift us. Life is precious – what are we going to use it for? If I use an iPhone as a door stopper it would probably work pretty well, but there's a hundred better things you can achieve with it. Human life is like that.

What if we are looking for help, but other spiritualists don't seem so forthcoming?

In spirituality, nobody is self-made and the assistance of others is essential. If we feel nobody is coming to help, there are certain things we can reflect upon.

Are we truly open to receiving help? Spiritual people tend not to impose themselves on others. They may not offer their advice and guidance unless they see someone is desirous, open and serious in applying that wisdom. Often times we are not looking for advice or help, but someone to reinforce our own views or ideas.

Are you fixed on where the help should come from? Providence will surely send help, but we may have a fixed idea of who we should receive help from. Sometimes we have to be open to the fact that certain people we'd like help from are not available, but there are many others who are willing and able to offer the same assistance.

Has the help already come, but maybe not in the way you would have expected or liked? Often times we have a fixed notion of what help means. Thus, many times help is manifesting in our life, but we can't see it because we have a stereotyped conception that we can't detach ourselves from.

How do we appropriately share spirituality in the world?

The first thing is that people don't care how much you know until they know how much you care. So the most basic way in which to help anyone in their life is to first become a good friend. Show them that you don't have an agenda above and beyond their own wellbeing. When they have confidence that you are genuinely interested in them, that you have the best intention in mind, then they'll be much more open to hearing you.

Secondly, we have to be a good example. St. Francis of Assisi once said, *"Preach the Gospel at all times and use words if necessary."* We can inspire people in spirituality without saying a word, because actions speak louder than words. Sometimes they say *"your character is speaking so loudly, I can't hear a word you're saying."*

Thirdly, when sharing knowledge, try to deeply understand the needs, interests and concerns of the people you are serving. Then, creatively demonstrate how spirituality addresses those needs on the deepest and most practical level. After all, everyone wants to know how this will tangibly help them in their life.

How can I stay enthusiastic when I don't feel appreciated in the community of spiritualists?

We all need appreciation, encouragement and empowering words. That gives us energy, faith and the enthusiasm to stride forward in our lives. But that is not the only ingredient.

Potters craft amazing artifacts using a special technique. One hand is placed inside the pot for support and the other hits the outside into shape! Genuine spiritual relationships embody appreciation but also critical feedback. There should be encouragement, but also challenge. There will be kind words and also cutting words when necessary. There should be support, but also moulding. That combination is essential.

Thus, when we continually look for appreciation and that becomes our prime meditation, we may find we become starved of it. More than appreciation, our main meditation should be improvement. When other spiritualists see that desire to improve they will invest in you with balanced doses of appreciation and correction, just like the brass potter.

Why is it so hard to accept the feedback or constructive criticism of others?

There are two fundamental blocks:

We can't see – it's difficult to see the picture when you're inside the frame. Entangled in our own emotions, perceptions, habits and opinions, we struggle to go beyond. A neutral observer can clearly see things that we are completely oblivious to. Our modes of functioning, however, become so engrained that we convince ourselves we must be right and conveniently disregard any opinions to the contrary.

We don't want to see – success, we feel, is to be 'perfect,' and when that perfection is questioned, our pride awakens to defend. More important than perfection, however, is progress. A spiritually successful day is one where we improve, refine and develop ourselves. How is that possible if we're unaware of our shortcomings? Stagnate in the illusion of perfection or progress in the reality of struggle – the choice is ours.

Even when feedback is out-and-out wrong, we'd do well to avoid disregarding it completely. Can we still learn a principle from what is being said? Even if the details are wrong, could the feedback apply to us in a different way? Can we take it as a timely warning of what not to do? Can we use their seemingly inaccurate analysis as an opportunity to exercise humility? All high ideals, I know, but that's what makes a sincere spiritualist so special. The great saints demonstrated how even the harsh criticism of an unreasonable faultfinder can enrich our spiritual growth, what to speak of the earnest words of concerned friends.

Do you have any tips on dealing with conflicts and disagreements?

Human relationships are riddled with quarrel and conflict. It's a symptom of the age. But that's not a problem per se since every disagreement is pregnant with positive and negative potential. Differences of opinion can bring enlightenment, transformation, wisdom and growth – they can also be the cause of anger, frustration, resentment and fall-out. Developing progressive responses in argumentative situations can be a liberating experience. Here are some tips:

Tolerance – the first moments of a conflict situation can determine the entire conversation. Be tolerant and patient. The art of conversation is not only to say the right thing at the right time but to leave unsaid the wrong thing at the tempting moments. Adopting an adversarial approach erects barriers which block the meeting of hearts.

Circumstance – beyond the perceived irrationality of actions and words, try to understand why someone is doing what they do. When you uncover the hidden story you hold the key to progress. In interpersonal relations, the golden rule is this: seek first to understand, then to be understood. To do that you have to listen with an open heart and an open mind.

Acceptance – did you ever consider that there may not be a right or wrong answer? Conflict comes from differences, but diversity is not necessarily bad. Fear of difference is fear of life itself. By accepting that we're all individuals, we can more fully appreciate that conflict is often a case of different 'angles of vision' illuminating the same truth.

Importance – keep disagreements in perspective and calmly evaluate their importance. Question whether the tenacious pursuance and resolution of a conflict is absolutely necessary. Many issues can easily be dropped or ignored, but often our emotional involvement keeps us doggedly fighting till the last breath.

Transcendence – we love to prove ourselves, but the spiritual principle is to transcend right and wrong. The real aim of an argument or discussion should not be victory, but progress. If a concession of 'defeat' improves our relationships, helps us develop character and opens up opportunities for progressive solutions, then where is the loss?

How can I effectively offer correction and feedback to someone else?

Life is replete with a plethora of opportunities to correct other people, and, truth be told, we do like to be right. The urge to offer feedback, however, must be exercised with caution.

Will they digest it? Even if you are right and even if your feedback is beneficial, deeply consider whether the person will actually be able to take it. When we know they can't digest it, yet our overwhelming urge drives us to force-feed them, we actually do a disservice. It's another type of violence because our inability to communicate appropriately can cement them further in their illusion. People raise their defences and become stubbornly unwilling to change. Remember that correcting someone is a service - its ultimate aim is to assist and encourage that person to grow.

Will you digest it? The process of correction can awaken our own pride and ego. As soon as we offer some words of advice, however true they may be, we automatically place ourselves in a superior position. We assume the position of a teacher. This sense of superiority can easily create an illusion and pride which diverts our attention from the internal upgrades that we require. Remember that correcting someone is a service and it should therefore facilitate the evolution of our own humility and progressive spiritual consciousness.

There you have the wrongs of being right - we neither helped the individual, nor did we help ourselves. Life is not about being right, it's about doing right. It's not simply an objective call, but an internal mood. They look similar but are oceans apart. Too many times we fall into the trap of being right, but doing wrong. It can break people, it can break us and it can break relationships. When issues need addressing, we should consider the array of alternative ways to 'get the message across'. Question is, do we have the patience, sensitivity and poise to employ them?

SELF DEVELOPMENT

Insightful urban gurus have shaped a new approach to life, reminding us of what lies beyond the routine agenda of eat, drink, be merry and enjoy. They teach us the five cardinal principles of happy marriage, the three ways to diffuse anger, the four steps to enduring vitality and the seven qualities that will win you the best friends on the planet; all of which help us craft more progressive, rewarding and happy lives.

Self-development has become one of the biggest industries of our time, promising to help us become the best versions of ourselves. While it promotes the ideals, we may question how much it actually equips and empowers one to genuinely imbibe this positive mental state. Can we psychologically convince ourselves to forgive others? Does genuine compassion and kindness towards the universe manifest on the level of the intellect? What part does spirituality play in self-development? In this section we explore the spiritual approach to help you sustainably live with these higher principles in mind.

Are self-development books useful in our spiritual journey?

Self-help is a booming industry – The Power of Now, The Seven Habits, The Alchemist, The Monk who sold his Ferrari, The Secret, The 5am Club... the list is endless and growing by the day! I would say many books give a lot of 'help' – practical tools, tips and life hacks that you can implement in the here and now. Often, however, they lack detailed understanding of the 'self' – substantial insight into consciousness and the workings of the body and mind in relation. Other books give philosophical insight into the 'self' but may not unpack that wisdom to give us the 'help' we need in practical, tangible and bite-size steps. The ultimate self-help must incorporate both aspects.

That's where the Bhagavad-gita really captured my imagination. The dialogue took place on a battlefield, which is actually a fascinating setting. On a battlefield there is an immediate sense of urgency, a pressure to act, function and respond – very much about the here-life. The battlefield also brings the after-life into question because death is the daily reality. Both aspects play on Arjuna's mind and Krishna beautifully unpacks how to live in the present and then integrate that into the bigger and broader journey of life. He brings together the practical and philosophical, the down-to-earth and transcendent, and seemlessly integrates them together.

Self-development is a natural consequence of spiritual development. Without genuine spirituality, self-development stagnates. Self-development without spiritual development lacks depth and sustainability. That doesn't mean we can't benefit from reading various books out there in the world, yet we must acknowledge their limitations. A change in our mindset and instinctive emotional response must come from a deeper transformation of consciousness. There has to be profound existential awakening. Only when we see our life situation as a chapter in a longer story, when we connect deeply with the divine intelligence who is behind the workings of nature and when we understand that we are spiritual beings on a human journey – only then can we function with genuine and sustained positivity.

How do I overcome procrastination?

First we have to understand where our procrastination stems from.

It could be a motivation problem. Only when our 'why' is deep enough, will our motivation to act be strong enough. When something has captured our imagination and ignited our enthusiasm, it generates a fire of desire that impels us out of the blocks. They say the best alarm clock in the world is purpose.

For others it may be a confidence problem. Even if we are motivated by something, we procrastinate when we lack the confidence and faith that we can achieve the goal. We have to believe it's possible. Due to fear of failure and embarrassment, many fail to even start the journey. Sometimes we can be our own self-destructive enemy.

Procrastination can also be connected to the environment. It's difficult to swim against the current and most people will just decide to give up. When the atmosphere around us is unsupportive and the people are sceptical, disempowering and negative, it can erode away our impetus to act.

Yet, even when we have the motivation, confidence and the right environment, if we are victimised by a lack of planning, coordination and organisation, that can also imprison us in procrastination. Often times we just don't know where to start, or we can't see how the defined activities will lead us to the goal. I personally keep a diary, plan my steps with short-term tasks and consciously integrate them into a long-term plan. Failing to plan means planning to fail.

Why do I have a chronic tendency to compare myself to others?

These are cancers of the mind: first we compare, then we compete, then we complain and eventually we criticise. It's a downward spiral. When we look at the tendency to compare, we see that it's rooted in two misconceptions. Firstly, we have the wrong *definition* of success and secondly, we have the wrong *approach* to success. If we correct these equations, we can free ourselves from comparison.

Our first pitfall is that we measure success in externals. How much someone earns, how beautiful someone looks, how popular and powerful they are. We measure someone's worth based on their power, position, prestige and popularity. Albert Einstein once said: *"Everything that can be counted doesn't necessarily count and that which can't be counted often counts for more."* Success is not in accolades or accomplishments, but lies in the internals – the effort, sincerity, intention and character that goes behind your noble endeavour. Once you have invested in that, you are already successful, regardless of the outcome. If we orient ourselves in this spiritual understanding, we avoid the impulsive and chronic tendency to constantly compare on externals.

Secondly, we have the wrong approach to success. The world, in gross and subtle ways, teaches us that if someone else is thriving, then that's reducing our opportunity for success. If someone has money, then that means it's money that I could have had. If someone has fame and attention, then it's attention that I have missed out on. In the materialistic approach our success is based on someone else's failure. Therefore, most people secretly enjoy seeing others fail because it

makes them feel more successful. In the spiritual sphere, however,
the parameters are entirely different. When you help someone
to be the best they can, you become the best you can. If you help
someone become wise in knowledge, you expand your understanding
automatically. If you try to help someone achieve their potential, you
blossom your own capacity. Thus, the success of someone else need
not threaten or depress us, but inspire and empower us.

I seem to keep encountering obstacles – what should I do?

Some people see problems in opportunities and others see
opportunities in problems – it all depends on vision. I'll tell you a story
to explain. A man of unbreakable determination resolved to climb
the peaks of the Himalayan ranges. After arriving at the foothills, he
checked into his hotel room in preparation for the arduous expedition
ahead. He rose the next morning, donned his mountaineering gear
and made his way to the hotel check-out. Upon reaching the reception
he peered outside and saw an aggressive snowstorm in bitingly cold
temperatures, with not a soul in sight. Undeterred and undaunted, he
handed his keys to the receptionist and headed straight for the door.
"Where are you going?!" the receptionist exclaimed, *"there's a weather
warning and hazardous conditions – nobody treks in such a situation!"*
Aware of the obvious obstacles, the trekker looked back with a sparkle
in his eye and replied, *"because my heart has already reached the peak,
there won't be any problem for my body to reach."* With those prophetic
words he ventured on, navigated the complexities and arrived at his
desired destination.

If your heart reaches, everything else falls into place. When we have
that determination, desire and rock-solid dedication, no external

obstacle can disable our progress. If we're convinced, nothing can derail us. Rather we'll see all the obstacles as stepping stones to success.

How can I discover my purpose and unique contribution in life?

Broadly speaking, three things are important.

Assess – reflect on your qualities and character, conduct a personality test and get to know yourself better. Try to identify those things you are good at and those things you are attracted to. The overlap of these two lists are certainly integral parts of your *dharma*, or unique purpose. Think about activities and situations in which you were naturally thriving. What are your strengths and weaknesses? What environments bring out the best in you? This kind of self-assessment can be very revealing.

Ask – draw upon the advice of friends, mentors and coaches. Sometimes our shyness and lack of confidence blocks our potential. Other times our desire to be like others veers us into an unnatural direction. We can't always analyse ourselves in an objective way, but neutral (and informed) observers can offer greater clarity and insight.

Attempt – try different things, explore and don't be afraid to fail. Take a course, learn new skills and embrace the unknown in a mood of discovery. Even when we attempt something and find it's not really suitable, it helps to point us in a more progressive direction. We should embrace the growth and wisdom that comes with so-called failure.

How can we stay positive and avoid disappointment?

Self Development

One medieval saint makes an interesting observation of the Bhagavad-gita. He points to one of the very first verses, where Krishna identifies Arjuna's lamentation and disappointment as illusory and needless (BG 2.11). In the very final verses of the Bhagavad-gita Krishna again implores Arjuna to give up his lamentation (BG 18.66). In both verses, *soca*, sadness or lamentation, appear, and the saintly commentator thus explains that the entire dialogue is based around lamentation because that is the basic human condition. Most people's lives are enveloped by different disappointments.

The entire dialogue of the Bhagavad-gita thus exists to address this inconvenient truth. Essentially, Krishna's entire task is to elevate Arjuna's vision. He wants Arjuna to see beyond the *senses* and his *sentiments* and thus introduces him to *scripture* which can empower one to see through the *soul*. When we have the bigger and broader picture, lamentation and disappointment, which exist due to a lack of perspective, immediately disappear. We have to develop the vision of eternity, deeply understanding that our current experiences are small chapters in a much longer story. We realise that all of the things that affect the body and mind may cause some pain, but don't need to create suffering, since we exist as an eternal soul, separate from these temporary conditions. We are on a bigger journey and beyond all of the ups and downs, we're heading towards something much better.

It's like an adult watching a child play a video game. While the kids shout, scream and focus the entirety of their emotions into it, the adult stands as an onlooker realising that it's all just virtual reality. The world is something like that. Ofcourse, when we go through the rollercoaster ride, we don't always perceive it like that and therefore having good friends who can lend us the bigger perspective is a saving grace.

4

How do we become humble and give up our ego?

In the strict sense ego means identity. We can't exist without identity, but we do want to shed the *false ego* – the idea that *"I'm the controller and enjoyer of everything I survey."* We may not overtly say that and neither ascribe to it, but deep within our psychology this conception takes root and taints our interactions with the world and everyone in it. Humility is the antidote – to somehow take ourselves out of the centre and learn to live with more selflessness and sensitivity.

How do we become humble? The great saint Bhaktisiddhanta Saraswati once said that *"Humility is the complete absence of the enjoying spirit."* That gave me the clue. I think the most practical way to develop humility is to always think about how to be a servant in every situation.

If you're a parent, then try to serve your children to be the best they can. If you're a child, then serve your parents in gratitude for everything they've done for you. When someone is going through pain, be a servant and try to help them find relief. When someone is trying to achieve something great in their life, be a servant and see how to assist them in that noble endeavour. Even leaders become servant-leaders to draw out the full potential of their subordinates.

When we constantly meditate on being a servant, we naturally become humble.

How do we stay free from temptation?

Oscar Wilde once said, *"I can resist everything except temptation!"* It is the great art of life – don't give up what you want most, for what feels good now. But, as we've all experienced, in the heat of the moment we often make the wrong decisions. The opportunity for instant gratification captures our mind and the urge within seems too powerful to tolerate. We know it would be a mistake, but we don't have the inner strength to say *"no."*

I often say that overcoming temptation will COST you:

Conviction – be convinced of the great thing you are trying to achieve and why it requires a certain discipline and self-restraint. Knowledge and clarity create immunity and inner strength. Here, we are focusing on the *intellectual level*.

Openness – regardless of success or failure, be open with a friend and seek their advice, support, guidance and feedback. Honesty will grow your character and integrity. This fortifies us on the *relationship level*.

Safety – avoid provoking places, people and objects that may compromise your principles. Don't fight battles that you don't need to. Strength comes from reorgainsing ourselves on the *practical level*.

Taste – work hard to experience the 'better life' and solidify your resolve by feeling the benefits of your restraint. Saturate your consciousness in something more progressive, pure and uplifting. This *spiritual level* is the safest platform from which temptation ultimately disappears.

How do we learn to adjust our expectations so we don't feel let down?

I don't think we can function in this world without some level of projection – we have to do some kind of pre-emptive thinking otherwise life would just be chaotic and unfruitful. We have to forecast, predict and naturally have a picture in our mind. I think the problems occur when our plans become expectations. Great expectations often lead to great frustrations.

Plans embody a certain amount of detachment because we know that the world is unpredictable. When we minus that detachment from our consciousness, our plans become expectations. We have a strong belief and desire that things will transpire in a certain way and haven't factored in the real possibility that things could go the other way. Plans never frustrate because from day one we accept that life never functions like clockwork.

When you have a plan you don't place all your hopes for happiness in that one basket. but when we have expectations we feel that happiness is dependent on a certain outcome.

When you have a plan you put the emphasis on the effort, endeavour and sincere attempt. When you have an expectation, you put the emphasis on the result, outcome and tangible end. Therefore, plans never frustrate you because once you've 'done your bit' you can rest assured that the outcome is divinely engineered and always for the good.

So, we can easily ask ourselves: *do I have plans or do I have expectations?* If you have plans you'll live a very progressive and positive life. Expectations, on the other hand, can limit you and lead to frustration and feelings of failure.

How do you cope with having demotivating and discouraging people around you?

First and foremost, make sure you have enough people in your life who are the exact opposite – people who encourage, uplift, support and lend you a vision of the brighter future. Even a few genuine people like that in your life is a great wealth. That positive energy and inspiring influence gives you an immunity from all the negative chatter. Everyone needs positive and progressive energy coming into their lives and when we receive it, we should diligently invest in those relationships. The greatest thing you can have is a person in your life who has more faith in you than yourself.

Secondly, realise that anyone who feels the need to look down upon, discourage or deflate another person is often experiencing a stagnancy in their own life. When people are not progressing, growing or evolving, they tend to drag other people back. Thus, any discouragement coming from them is more a reflection of that person's own weakness and difficulty, rather than yours.

Thirdly, use the criticisms and comments of others to nourish your own self-awareness. Question whether there is any value or insight in their comments and critiques. Our greatest critics can sometimes utter a grain of truth and lend useful insight. Even if there is no truth in what they say, take it that they are warning you of what not to do in the future!

Finally, when people look down on you, use it as an opportunity to develop your internal muscles of tolerance and humility. Without these challenging people in our life, the resistance which helps us to develop deeper character is absent. Every time we encounter these situations or personalities, we use it as an opportunity - *"You've come today as a messenger of the Divine to teach me qualities which will aid my spiritual journey."* Srila Prabhupada famously writes: *"One's greatness is measured by their ability to tolerate provoking situations."*

How can I embrace the risks that will allow me to grow?

It requires a shift of mindset. Instead of constantly being nervous about everything that could go wrong, we need to start getting excited about everything that could go right. For example, when you're preparing to address an audience, there is a certain energy that runs though you. Now, if you're meditating on how you may fail, you'll turn up on the stage full of nervousness and apprehension. If you're visualising the beautiful contribution you can make in a spirit of service, you'll turn up excited and enthused. Same energy, different mindset, opposite results.

Here is another perspective: doubting is as risky as doing. Did you know that? Often, we procrastinate and hesitate because we have doubts and we generally think 'holding back' is the safe option. That's not the case, since doubting and doing are both as risky as each other.

Some months ago, I entered the renounced order of life. Later, someone approached me and said, *"but it's such a risk, a lifetime vow, a bold step to take."* I replied to them saying *"yes it is a risky decision - but not embracing renunciation is also a risk, getting married is also a risk, not getting married is also a risk - doing anything is a risk and not doing anything is also a risk!"* There's something inbuilt within us by which we consider that not doing something is always safer than doing something. That's not the case. Not doing the right thing is as risky as doing the wrong thing.

We have to also learn to doubt our doubts. I'm not suggesting you become kamikaze and just start making all kinds of bold decisions. Naturally, there's a voice of reason and doubts are there to help us think deeper about our decisions. If we're constantly jarred by doubts, however, we can't move forward. It's like trying to drive a car with your foot on the brake pedal. You're not going to hit anything, but you're definitely not going to reach anywhere either!

How can we avoid getting into arguments?

Human relationships are riddled with quarrel and conflict. Differences of opinion, however, can bring enlightenment, transformation, wisdom and growth - they can also be the cause of anger, frustration, resentment and fall-out. Developing progressive responses in times of disagreement is a most rewarding experience.

I do entire sessions on conflict resolution but let me share one thing that you may find helpful.

Once, a man came to his minister venting that his wife is always complaining and criticising, perpetually raising problems and issues. *"I'm not an argumentative person"* he said, *"but she just draws me into that space."* The minister advised him to *"go back and listen to every single word she's saying very carefully, without replying."* He dutifully did that, returned to his minister and said *"her words make no sense to me, and to be honest I now feel even more angry!"* The minister then told him, *"now I want you to go back and listen to everything she's **not** saying."* He was puzzled! How do you listen to something that someone's not saying? The minister wanted to train him to hear the unheard.

It worked. The man came back and told the minister - *"even though what she says seems illogical, unreasonable and impulsive, I can better understand where she is coming from."* We must listen closely to people's hearts, hearing their feelings uncommunicated, pains unexpressed and complaints unaddressed. Relationships break down when we impulsively react to someone else's superficial words and instinctive actions. We must penetrate beyond so we can ascertain the true opinions, feelings and desires of the people we relate to. Then we achieve substantial growth and make real progress.

How do you develop compassion?

Real compassion arises in a heart which is deeply fulfilled. Generally, because we have a vacuum within our own hearts, it's very difficult to be kind and generous with others. But when you are feeling spiritual nourishment and genuine inner connection, then you can naturally give yourself freely to others without consideration of return. That's the platform of deep compassion.

Until we reach that elevated point, we try to at least culture a mood of giving. We seem to perpetually retreat back into the comfort of our own selfish world, and in those times we remind ourselves to continue venturing out and helping others. Selfless service brings a reciprocation which catapults us to higher experiences of Divinity.

Do you have any practical guidance on gratitude?

Srila Prabhupada would say that first we have to become conscious, then we can become spiritually conscious. In this regard, the 'five finger prayer' reminds us of various people who should appear in our consciousness regularly.

The **thumb** represents those who are closest to you. They are the pillars in your life, the loved ones who have been with you through thick and thin. They're the first people you should be conscious of and sensitive to and the first ones you should offer gratitude to and pray for.

The **first finger** represents your teachers and instructors, who offered guidance, instruction, inspiration and direction. They are the one's who mould you, train you and provide you with the resources and wisdom to help you build your life.

The third and **tallest finger** represents the leaders in your life. For us to grow, many people around us took responsibility and made sacrifices. Some of them you may have met and probably many of them you haven't. Spiritual role models and community leaders are very good examples. Each generation stands taller than the previous, because they stand on the shoulders of the previous generation.

Then there is the **weak finger** which represents the people around you who are vulnerable and in need of protection and support. Sometimes we forget about the suffering unless they're on our doorstep. We can offer prayers for their upliftment, wellbeing and prosperity.

The **smallest finger** represents yourself. We can also introspect and feel grateful for the opportunities we have had in our spiritual journey. We can pray to improve and become more established in living our ideals.

How can I overcome regrets in my life?

How wonderful if we could live a life without any regrets. One of my mentors would often say, *"The pain of discipline is uncomfortable, but the pain of regret is unbearable."* One of the great arts of life is to find the courage, discipline and determination that drives us toward our full potential.

That said, you'd be hard pushed to find someone in this world who doesn't have any regrets. When we find those regrets within us, here are some things to ponder over so you can frame them appropriately:

Illusory – regret is generated in our minds because we are comparing to an ideal. The difference between the real and the ideal can cause regret, since it conjures up feelings of failure. Often times, however, that ideal may not be realistic and if that's the case, then our regret is illusory. We are often comparing what has happened to a scenario that likely would never happen.

Imbalaced – often times we regret a certain decision or direction without seeing the full picture. We don't always see that the choice and direction we embraced also brought certain gifts in our life. We tend to see only what we missed out on, but not on what we received.

Informative – regrets are powerful if they inform us about a better way to live. Sometimes this is the only way in which we learn to upgrade our approach to life. If something brings progression, development and evolution, it's not to be lamented.

PRACTICAL SPIRITUALITY

In numerous scriptures, the great teachers have detailed a scientific process of devotional practice that culminates in divine love. Daily, regulated, devotional acts, (in Sanskrit, sadhana-bhakti) lead to mystical, individual spontaneity (in Sanskrit, raganuga-bhakti).

Along with these spiritual practices there are recommendations on lifestyle and habits which support and empower one's spiritual endeavours. While living in the world, the spiritualist has to seamlessly integrate spirituality into their daily functioning and that is not always easy. There are obstacles and complexities, opposition and distraction. The spiritualist can sometimes feel like they're swimming against the tide, with the odds stacked against them. In this section we explore some of the frequent inquiries related to practicing spirituality in the modern world and unpack useful insights to support you on that journey.

I appreciate spirituality, but why do I have to be part of an organised religion?

Well, we studied at an organised school, we buy things at an organised shopping center, we fly the world from organised airports and when we're sick, we got to an organised hospital. The moment these things become disorganised we become frustrated to no end. Imagine driving on a disorganised road (and if you've never experienced that, just go to India and find out!). It's clear that organisation brings many benefits that we deeply appreciate. Yet we also know that organisation in a religious institution can lead to dilution, deviation and even degradation.

Bhaktisiddhanta Saraswati Thakur said the institution of religion was a *"necessary evil."*

Evil because it can easily become about power, position, politics, popularity and prestige, while genuine spirituality and the essence falls by the wayside. Organised religion can promote membership over friendship, doctrine over dialogue, numbers over faces, holiness over humanity, the after-life over the here-life. History has shown how religious traditions often become mechanical, ritualistic and permeated by blind adherence to generational customs. For most people, that's a major turn off.

Bhaktisiddhanta Saraswati also said it was necessary. Without the spiritual company of other sincere seekers, where do we find the support, strength, encouragement and inspiration to reach our full spiritual potential? Organised communities where people come together for a common purpose is an essential part of any human endeavour. There is strength in numbers and also invaluable opportunities for growth and discovery.

The spiritual journey of Krishna Consciousness goes through various stages which leave no 'holes' of doubt:

H – Hear – the practitioner first focuses on hearing and digesting the philosophy. Far from a call for blind faith, the spiritualist is encouraged to investigate whether the philosophy makes logical sense and is comprehensive enough to address the multifarious aspects of reality that we see before us.

O – Observe – next, we begin to deeply look at the world through the lens of that philosophy and see whether it helps us uncover answers to the questions that sit deep within our hearts. We can also test whether the philosophy and wisdom we are hearing tally's with the real-world situations we observe around us every day.

L – Live – when we have a higher degree of faith, we can begin implementing the spiritual practices and processes that are recommended in the body of teachings. We make those devotional acts a part of our life and begin to explore it beyond just 'the head.'

E – Experience – that practice, coupled with the appropriate lifestyle and culture, will trigger divine connection and tangible experience. We begin to perceive spirituality as something more than just theoretical and ethereal – but as substantial and real.

S – Serve – having experienced the efficacy of the process, the spiritualist seeks to selflessly share their experiences with the objective of making the world a happier and healthier place. This spirit of service confirms and further amplifies our experience of the spiritual reality.

Is it as objective and solid as mainstream science?

Are you sure that modern science is as objective and solid as you think?

Firstly, it's not that everything we read about in textbooks, hear about in lecture theatres and see advertised in the world as conclusive, has actually been proven beyond doubt. Many things the scientific community boldly present to the world are very much theories and based on blatent underlying faith.

Secondly, we find an irrational stubbornness in science which holds onto certain viewpoints and theories even when clear evidence comes to light that runs contrary. We see a 'knowledge filter' in society whereby evidence and findings which don't support the prevailing paradigm are masked from public view.

Thirdly, modern science is often surrounded by artficial hype and scientists often inflate their explanatory power beyond what has been rightfully earned. Their ability to manipulate and simulate certain aspects of the world shouldn't be extrapolated to an unreasonable degree.

Some may say that the practice of spiritual science requires some faith, but those who follow mainstream materialistic science invest the same faith in their accepted worldview.

What are the Bhagavad-gita's insights on stress management?

A quick flick through some Sanskrit verses of the Bhagavad-gita immediately reveal three common reasons why our consciousness diverges into this uncomfortable emotional state:

Regulation – Gita insights (Chapter 6, Verse 17) reveal that regulated habits of eating, sleeping, work and recreation counteract all physical and mental pain. An imbalanced lifestyle blinds us from knowing our limits, drawing us into dangerous territory that we can't navigate. Know your boundaries. Pushing beyond one's comfort zone and venturing into the unknown is admirable, but too much irregularity will begin 'bending' and eventually end-up 'breaking' you. Be dynamic and daring, but maintain your balance and strength through regulation.

Expectation – Gita insights (Chapter 2, Verse 47) remind us to perform our duty, but simultaneously remain detached from the results. All said and done, we are not the controller. When we formulate ambitious hopes on what we'll achieve and how life will transpire, we carry a burden of expectation that is unsustainable. It's commendable to have plans and aspirations and it's healthy to strive hard for them, but once we've tried our best, we must step back, disconnect and remain detached. When 'plans' turn into 'expectations' we set ourselves up for misery.

Competition – Gita insights (Chapter 3, Verse 35) guide us to perform our own *dharma* (purpose) instead of someone else's. Being ourselves is more productive, joyful and sustainable. Unfortunately, we tend to measure our worth by comparing ourselves with others. We forget that we're on our own path, with our own obstacle course and our own unique calling. Comparison clouds our original thinking and blocks our distinctive contribution. As Albert Einstein said: *"Everybody is a genius, but if you judge a fish by its ability to climb a tree, it will live its whole life believing that it is stupid."*

Overcoming stress, then, is quite simple: *maintain your regulation, adjust your expectation and drop the competition.*

How can we make good decisions in life?

Firstly, try to ensure that your decisions reflect your dreams and not your fears. We often make decisions based on what we fear could go wrong. That may save us from some problem, but it definitely won't transport us to our full potential. Average decisions are primarily founded upon fears, whereas amazing decisions are based on dreams. We acknowledge fears without being limited and choked by them.

Secondly, don't just make decisions which will please people in the immediate, but those which will genuinely serve and enrich them in the long run. We look for acceptance, acknowledgement and appreciation, but we should deeply think how we can do the best for them in the bigger picture. Sometimes we have to take bold decisions (which often meet with opposition) that will serve others in a much more valuable way.

Thirdly, there is a temptation to make decisions based on impulse and intuition, but the best decisions also incorporate inspiration and guidance. We have to follow our heart's calling, but hearing from others can often help us better identify that inner calling. Just like Arjuna, who turned to Krishna for guidance, we have the opportunity to get feedback on our intentions from spiritual books and spiritual friends.

Is nostalgia bad?

We have to be careful.

Psychologists have often talked about something called the 'peak-end principle.' Often, when we reflect on the past, we tend to focus on the peak emotions of that time and also the final emotion we were left

with of that time. Everything else gets somewhat side-lined. Thus, if
a time was overall very good and productive, but there were specific
moments of intense difficulty, or if the end was very painful, we tend
to frame the whole time period in that way and remember it like that.
The opposite also happens. Thus, our assesment and analysis of the
past is quite often inaccurate.

Even when our analysis of the past is accurate and positive, we
still have to be careful. Looking back and having fond memories is
something we all do and there is no crime in that. We do, however,
have to be careful of two things. Firstly, there is a tendency to convince
ourselves that previous situations were much better, leaving us feeling
dissatisfied and demotivated. Secondly, our preoccupation with the
past can prevent us from designing the future and focusing on the
potential of the beautiful times ahead.

To think, learn and be inspired by the past is commendable, but to live
in the past is debilitating.

What is the best lifestyle for a spiritualist?

In the 14th, 17th and 18th chapters of the Bhagavad-gita, Krishna discusses
the 'Three Modes of Material Nature.' He explains that everything in
existence is coloured by a combination of these three energies and
our inner disposition is similarly influenced. A detailed description
of the three energies, known as goodness, passion and ignorance, are
given: what their symptoms are, and how they influence and affect our
approach to life.

For example, Krishna explains how the foods we eat can be in ignorance,
passion, or goodness. He also explains how our sense of happiness,
one's determination and the charity we offer can be in different

modes. By hearing these various examples we begin to understand the principles of each mode of nature. When we absorb that wisdom, we can pratically see how everything we do in life and everything we engage with, is tainted by these influences. From the way someone parents their children, to how they drive their car, to their sleeping patterns and study habits – it's all influenced by goodness, passion or ignorance, and usually a combination of them all.

Thus, Krishna opens up the opportunity to be more mindful of the habits, lifestyles and ways in which we function. When we embrace goodness in all aspects of our life there are many benefits: one's physical and mental health improves, we develop better character and qualities, relationships tend to thrive and overall, we are able to achieve more and reach our potential. When we live in goodness our overall sense of happiness increases and it provides the best platform from which to practice deeper spirituality.

What was your first profound experience in spirituality?

It's hard to convey a profound experience because that's a very internal thing. I will, however, share some experiences on my spiritual journey that really stood out for me.

The first time I read the Bhagavad-gita was profound, but not for the reasons you may imagine. I opened the book in great anticipation that many mysteries would now unfold before my eyes. After a few pages of reading, however, I closed the book because practically everything was incomprehensible to me. Interestingly, I was still super inspired because something within me had grasped the fact that I had contacted profound wisdom, but it would only be accessible through the help of established teachers. The knowledge and words seemed to be touching another part of my existence beyond the mind and intellect. It was the first time I had read something and been inspired without even understanding it!

Another notable experience was the first time I danced while chanting the Hare Krishna mantra. I tend to be quite introvert, reserved, shy and generally very quiet. In *kirtan* (congregational chanting) I usually stayed in the back, observed others, keeping a distance from the dancing, which to me was out of my comfort zone. In one particular event, however, I remember how I almost instantaneously lost that inhibition and started dancing. That was interesting because nothing in my life had previously impelled me to 'go beyond my mind' in that way and transcend my self-consciousness. I knew this was something powerful.

Japa, mantra meditation on beads, has also been very uplifting for me. Though I won't testify to divine encounters and mystical visions of God, there have been numerous times in chanting when I felt completely in the moment – a sense of absolute liberation from past or future. For something so seemingly simple to capture my mind and lock me into the moment so profoundly, amazed and astounded me.

Another beautiful experience in my life was going to Vrindavana, the sacred village where Krishna was present generations ago. It's said that when we visit such places, we are actually returning to our eternal home, the place where we feel most natural and comfortable. In Vrindavana I found myself most happy in a 'normal way!' Usually happiness comes from an achievement, a unique experience, an unexpected fortune or a break from the norm. In Vrindavana, however, I felt a different type of happiness which was based on complete simplicity and spiritual connection, such that external conditions seemed inconsequential.

Like this, over the years, there have been numerous other experiences. I'm not claiming them all to be deeply spiritual in nature, but definitely indicators for me of a different reality. Krishna Consciousness is like an ocean and once you dive in, you start encountering more and more. You remain an eternal student, waiting for the next revelation of Divinity.

How can I deepen my spirituality?

Spiritual life is nourished through five principles - A, B, C, D, E. If you make these five things a part of your daily life, you will see incredible progress on your journey – tried and tested!

A stands for **Association**. We all need friends. On the journey of life there are twists and turns, ditches and dead ends, obstacles and opposition. But as John Lennon sang *"I get by with a little help from my friends."* Those who embark on the spiritual journey are brave indeed. They strive for purity in a world of degradation, they embrace simplicity amongst rampant materialism and they cultivate selflessness in an atmosphere charged with exploitation. Anyone who boldly goes against the grain will face temptation, doubt, ridicule and moments of weakness. Without the encouragement, support and good advice of spiritual friends how can one continue? Srila Prabhupada established ISKCON (International Society for Krishna Consciousness) to give people the chance to develop relationships with devotees of Krishna. This is one of the most effective ways to gain faith and become enthusiastic in spiritual life.

B stands for **Books**. Krishna explains that there is nothing in this world as sublime as transcendental knowledge. Firstly, knowledge is compared to a sword which cuts down our doubts and helps one remain determined and confident in their spiritual quest. Secondly, knowledge is likened to a lamp which warns us of the obstacles and impediments that we may encounter in our lives. Thirdly, knowledge is compared to a boat which protects one from the sufferings of this oceanic world and simultaneously carries one to the spiritual realm, face-to-face with Krishna. When Srila Prabhupada spoke into a Dictaphone and translated the timeless wisdom of the Vedas, Lord Krishna and the great teachers spoke through him. That spiritual sound was then transformed into the printed word, which, when read and assimilated, can once again manifest the full potency of the original sound.

C stands for **Chanting.** Five hundred years ago, Krishna incarnated as Sri Chaitanya Mahaprabhu and ushered in a spiritual revolution by freely initiating everyone – regardless of race, religion, or social status – into the chanting of the most effective *mantra* of all, the Hare Krishna *mantra.* Since God is all-powerful and all-merciful, He has kindly made it very easy for us to chant His names and He has also invested all His powers in them. Thus, the vibrated names of God and God Himself are identical. This means that when we chant the holy names of Krishna we are directly associating with Him and simultaneously being purified by such communion. Chanting is a prayer to Krishna that means *"O energy of the Lord (Hare), O all-attractive Lord (Krishna), O supreme enjoyer (Rama), please engage me in Your service."* This chanting is exactly like the genuine cry of a child for its mother's presence.

Hare Krishna Hare Krishna Krishna Krishna Hare Hare / Hare Rama Hare Rama Rama Rama Hare Hare

D stands for **Diet.** The Bhagavad-gita proclaims eating to be an extremely sacred activity when practiced with due care, attention and spiritual consciousness. If we place an iron rod in a fire, soon the rod becomes red hot and acts just like fire. In the same way, food prepared for and offered to Krishna with love and devotion becomes completely spiritualised. Such food is called Krishna prasadam, which means 'the mercy of Lord Krishna.' Eating prasadam is a fundamental practice of *bhakti-yoga.* In other forms of yoga one must artificially repress the senses, but the *bhakti-yogi* can engage his or her senses in a variety of pleasing spiritual activities.

E stands for **Engage**. We all have the opportunity to engage our talents, abilities, interests and time in practical service to God and the world. Spirituality is about selfless giving and when we take the opportunity to engage in service without expectation, this is known as bhakti, or devotional service. It can be anything from cooking, cleaning, driving, organising, counselling... we find ourselves by thinking of others.

Do you have any tips on time management?

Years ago, the main approach to time management was that of the **maximisers**. Their approach was to organise things in such a way so you can fit as much as possible into your life. Later, the **prioritisers** added more to the discussion. They said it's not just about doing more things, but it's about doing the most important things. Their approach was to prioritise and establish first things first. Down the line came the **eliminators**. They said the key to time management is not just about what you do, but identifying and eliminating what you don't have to do. If we don't consciously cross things off the list, some things will inevitably and inadvertently get left out.

All of these approaches have their merits. Krishna, in the Bhagavad-gita adds another perspective – the **multiplier** approach. Here, we see how to structure life in such a way that a single activity achieves multiple purposes. We tend to compartmentalise our life, especially when it comes to spirituality. Material responsibilities and spiritual aspirations, however, can be integrated.

For example, you have to do exercise, but you could potentiality incorporate spirituality into it by perhaps listening to something uplifting while you do it. Everyone has to cook and eat, but if you offer that meal to God, it becomes a spiritual activity. You have duties as a husband, wife, parent – but can you be a spiritual husband, a spiritual wife, a spiritual parent – by incorporating spirituality into the relationship? At the end of the Bhagavad-gita Krishna tells us that whatever we do in life can be done as a spiritual activity if we have the proper consciousness and orientation.

If we can somehow craft a life in which our aspirations integrate, we will find that our time expands.

Why do we sometimes feel stagnant in our lives?

Observing my own life, it seems there are three 'usual suspects' that stifle our growth and development. We slide into mediocrity when we are too busy, too arrogant or too comfortable to invest in our development. Growth consists of these key ingredients:

Time – our valuable hours are consumed by pressing issues and daily demands. Some things surely require immediate attention, but we have a chronic tendency to unnecessarily promote tasks in our 'to-do list' that may well be urgent but not really very important. Thus, we end up neglecting that which doesn't frantically tag on our consciousness, but which is key to the bright future ahead – time spent reflecting, planning, exploring and questioning. We need to free up tangible time and mental space to 'think out of the box.'

Humility – to improve, we must first acknowledge we are not the best version of ourselves. This requires humility. Our pride convinces us that we've found the best way to function. We think ourselves one step ahead of everyone else and it's difficult to see how we could be wrong.

A humble person accepts their limitations and looks for guidance, ever seeking an opportunity to refine and enhance their character and lifestyle.

Courage – life is a perennial tension between comfort and aspiration. We seek to explore, to grow, to achieve, yet we also desire security, safety and certainty. Truth be told, we have to sacrifice one to get the other. If we opt to remain in the comfort-zone, we may have to live with the inevitable feelings of being humdrum, run-of-the-mill and unexciting. On the other hand, if we dive for our dreams, we'll have to ready ourselves to brave the rocky road of uncertainty and opposition. Every significant achievement has its price tag. In an age where security, establishment and balanced prosperity have become the prevailing markers of a successful life, only a few have the courage to follow their dreams.

How can I become more confident?

The modern self-development gurus teach us that confidence comes from within. You have to 'believe in yourself.' If you are sure, others will be sure – your consciousness creates the reality. They tell us to be optimistic about our abilities, to pride ourselves in our strengths and to have the conviction that anything is possible if we try hard enough. This 'material confidence' may work in a limited scope for a short time. Such confidence, however, which is rooted in self-assurance, will gradually deflate. We eventually realise that we're not what we pumped ourselves up to be. In his prime, Muhammed Ali proudly asserted: *"I am the greatest!"* Later in life he realised his folly and declared himself the greatest fool for having wildly overestimated his position.

Real confidence comes from humility. We realise our inherent limitations, but gain firm conviction from knowing that the all-powerful will of providence is on our side. With such transcendental backing, anything is possible. For one who is 'quietly confident', their surety is grounded in humility and dependence and they can thus achieve unimaginable things in this world. Pride, complacency and hopelessness are not found in their dictionary. Seeing themselves as merely instruments, their job is to remove their ego from the situation and let the divine magic manifest.

Why doesn't God answer my prayers?

On my travels I once met a lady who told me her story: two years of spiritual travels, countless nights of prayer, careful scriptural exploration and persistent introspection, but still no sign! *"Will I ever find Him?"* she asked. *"I'm beginning to question whether He even exists."* What to speak of the 'searchers,' even the faithful often doubt that God is actually alive and active. A seeming lack of reciprocation and intervention can discourage even the most devout spiritualist. Where is God when you need Him?

While desiring a divine audience, we'd do well to bear the following in mind:

Action – internal yearning should be accompanied by external endeavour. When the man made a diligent daily prayer to win the lottery, God was more than willing to acquiesce – if only he actually went out and bought a ticket. Thus, it could also be that God wants to see a practical demonstration of our eagerness to see Him. What are we willing to sacrifice and what tangible efforts will we make to search Him out?

Reaction – we are not dealing with a cosmic order-supplier, but with a person. As persons, we don't mechanise our reciprocation, but rather operate on the basis of feelings and inspiration. Thus, one cannot force open the doors to see God, but should rather humbly engage themselves with enthusiasm and determination. We should eagerly anticipate a divine audience, but simultaneously be willing to patiently wait.

Perception – maybe God has already intervened in our life, but not in the way we were expecting. Often times we don't see things as they are, but rather we see things as we are. When we carry stereotyped perceptions of how God should deal with us, we leave little room to witness how He is expertly working on a bigger and better plan that will satisfy our needs and desires on the deepest level.

How can I detect that I have become mechanical and ritualistic in my spirituality?

Here are some classic symptoms of mechanical spirituality:

- I 'fit in' my practices as opposed to prioritising a suitable time of day

- I 'multi-task' my practices as opposed to giving them exclusive focus and attention

- I have no serious plans (or desires) to increase and enhance my practices

- I look for excuses and justification to neglect my spiritual practices

- I lack quality remembrance of the goal and purpose while performing my spiritual practices

- The mind frequently wanders during my practices and I happily let it travel

When we neglect to invest quality time and consciousness into performing the simple acts of devotion, we start tending towards being ritualistically religious rather than dynamically spiritual.

What signs indicate advancement in spirituality?

When hungry people sit down to eat a sumptuous meal, you can be sure that certain things will transpire. The initial feeling is one of pleasure. A well-cooked meal gives an immediate sense of enjoyment to the palate. Secondly, we feel nourishment and revitalisation of the body with each bite. Finally, our hunger gradually subsides and a disinterest and detachment from whatever other food preparations may be on offer, naturally arises.

In the same way the hungry spiritualist should feel three main things as they diligently apply themselves to the spiritual process. Firstly, there should be an immediate sense of happiness, quite different from anything experienced in the mundane realm. It's a feeling which is deeper, sustained and not dependent on external factors. Secondly, there should be nourishment of the soul which comes in the form of a direct experience of Divinity. One sees amazing opportunity and meaning everywhere and life becomes infused with hope, seeing providential arrangements behind everything. Finally, one will experience an increasing disinterest and detachment from temporary material goals that people frantically sacrifice and strive for. Even when material temptations flow into their mind, they remain undisturbed, convinced that there is something beyond.

PHILOSOPHY & THEOLOGY

If you imagine all knowledge to be contained within a circle, then one small part of that circle is "what you know." A slightly bigger portion is "what you know, you don't know." The largest part of the circle, however, is "what you don't know, you don't know." In other words, there is so much untapped wisdom out there that we're completely unaware of – wisdom which can dramatically shift our paradigms and awaken us to truths of a higher nature.

We all have inquiries and questions which sit deep within us, but society has trained us to side-line them and instead focus on immediate, tangible pursuits. We're told that those inquiries are unanswerable and unknowable and that spending time in exploration will only frustrate and obstruct us. In this section we explore the philosophical perspectives and theological concepts that stem from the Vedic literatures, summarised in the Bhagavad-gita. We get a glimpse of how comprehensive, empowering and beautiful the insights are and how patient comprehension of them can empower our life in all ways.

If God exists, wouldn't it be so blatantly obvious that nobody could miss it?

It's actually an amazing exhibition of God's ingenuity to create the possibility of atheism. God designs the world in such a way that people can argue Him out of the equation! He leaves room for explanations that (at least externally) seem to coherently explain the universe in purely mechanistic terms. In other words, He doesn't make it a completely ludicrous proposition to not believe in Him.

There is an element of force in intellectually cornering someone. If you were obliged to believe in something it would be difficult to simultaneously pour your heart into it. Thus, since God is ultimately interested in pure and unmotivated loving relationships, He endows us with independence and offers an array of options. That said, He does also present a persistent spiritual philosophy, which cements His ontological position as God in no uncertain terms. Ancient scriptures provide an in-depth analysis of creation, consciousness and the workings of Mother Nature. They clearly establish that belief in a higher reality is scientifically credible and logically coherent.

Can God create a rock so heavy that He can't lift it?

This question, coined the 'problem of rocks' supposedly exposes the paradoxicality of omnipotence, or the existence of an all-powerful entity. The theist is presented with a dilemma: Can God create a rock so heavy that He cannot lift it? If God can create a rock that is so heavy that He cannot lift it, then there is something that He cannot do, namely lift the rock in question. If God cannot create a rock that is so heavy that He cannot lift it, then there is something that He cannot do, namely create such a rock. Therefore, either way, God falls short and if there is something that He cannot do, then can He really be considered omnipotent? Clever argument.

While many philosophers attempt to deconstruct the riddle with creative linguistics, the saint Prabhupada had his own original response. When representatives from MENSA posed the same question to him in the 1970s, Prabhupada's answer was simple, yet profound – *"Yes, He can indeed create a rock so heavy that He cannot lift it... but then He can lift it!"* That was the end of that conversation!

The world we live in is characterised by boundaries, quantities and restrictions. Therefore, we tend to approach the Divine with these same boxed conceptions and thus fail to recognise that the spiritual reality is beyond the dimensional limits that define our daily functioning. In the spiritual strata, power is not static, but ever increasing. Personality is ever developing. The relationships are ever fresh and the happiness derived from such interactions is like an ever expanding ocean. Thus, since there is nothing static about the spiritual paradigm, it will always prove problematic to try and box it within a material construct.

How do you respond to religions who say they are the only way?

Vedic teachers explain that the various religious traditions all stem from a divine source and all offer the potential of spiritual elevation. The differences between them are primarily in culture, ritual and expression, while the core principles remain universal. Since the same message was taught in different times, places and circumstances, the externals had to be adapted – essentially, old wine in new bottles. Every religion can give you spiritual benefit, every religion can connect you to God and every religion can help you progress on your journey back to the spiritual realm, providing it's practiced with sincerity and purity.

Why then, one may ask, did I choose to follow this particular path? That's where theology gets interesting! Though there is unity in diversity, the variation between religions also represents an evolution of thought. While it would be unreasonable to claim one religion has a monopoly on spirituality, it's also inaccurate to claim that they're all identical. Rather, theologies differ in their detail of philosophical description, in their applicability and relevance over changing times, in their beauty and poetic charm and in the way they tangibly transform the practitioner. On these counts, my personal study of philosophy and theology led me to the conclusion that the Bhagavad-gita is outstanding and unique. It has thus been the focus of my attention, study and spiritual inspiration for over two decades.

How do we reconcile differences in philosophy and theology between religions?

Here are some reasons we may perceive 'differences' between theologies:

Context – religious scriptures and statements must be understood in relation to the entire body of teachings and with due consideration of the social context within which they were presented. 'Differences' may be perceived because we adopt a one-dimensional approach i.e., taking statements simplistically, without understanding the context, purpose and background behind them.

Emphasis – different traditions and teachers may stress and highlight different things. Our spiritual evolution requires systematic refinement of character and consciousness and different traditions may well work on different aspects of this. Thus, they may emphasise different points, but such 'differences' are a part of a broader harmony and evolution.

Interpretation – we understand the divine traditions through the representatives of that faith. While this is perfectly appropriate, the teachers have to prove themselves as transparent and free from the propensity to posit their own ideas. 'Differences' may surface because we mistake human opinions as gospel truths.

Authority – any religious claims must be traceable back to the original texts. In today's world, much confusion ensues due to a lack of reference to authentic scripture. People claim to speak for a tradition yet offer no reference point for their presentation. Thus, 'differences' may well be due to inaccurate and erroneous presentations which veer away from authentic theology.

Why should I take the Bhagavad-gita seriously?

Some years ago, the American Psychologist William James claimed that although there are a multitude of options in life, certain opportunities stand out above the rest due to key factors:

- **Practical** – I can do it (without harmful consequences and drastic changes to my life)

- **Beneficial** – I want to do it (because there is intrinsic logical value in this option)

- **Probable** – I feel confident to do it (since many people have experienced the benefit)

If something is practical, beneficial and probable, it's considered a 'live option,' and it's in our self-interest to invest time and energy into seriously considering it. To whimsically reject such opportunities would be irrational, unintelligent and unjustifiable. If there is something that could enhance your life, that is easily applicable and is something that many people are clearly benefitting from, why would you not at least explore it?

If we objectively analyse wisdom traditions and spiritual paths it becomes strikingly obvious that they fulfil such criteria. The Bhagavad-gita propounds a spiritual practice that is incredibly practical, not requiring massive lifestyle changes, but simple additions of yoga and meditation into one's daily routine. There are huge benefits on a physical, emotional and spiritual level that make logical sense and become quite apparent within a short time. Millions of people esteem the profundity of the Bhagavad-gita and gain immense spiritual wisdom and inner peace from its teachings.

While one may not want to blindly follow it, surely it would be just as absurd to blindly doubt it. To categorically deny such traditions, such live options, without any significant investigation, suggests a stubborn, irrational and illogical predisposition towards a certain worldview. Ironically, the very individuals who reject such traditions without thorough investigation, simultaneously pride themselves in being 'scientific' and 'free from subjective superstition'!

What are the top five life-changing verses from the Gita?

We are all individuals and we all have our individual journeys. When you read the Bhagavad-gita, specific things will touch your heart and feel incredibly relevant, inspiring and powerful to you. I have my verses that I go back to again and again and you will naturally find yours! Let me tell you a story from the Muslim Sufi tradition.

A disciple once approached his Sufi teacher with a request: *"Master, I heard you've gathered many jewels from the scriptures – can I acquire some of them?"* The master paused, reflected and finally replied: *"if I sell you those jewels you won't be able to afford them, and if I give you them for free you won't appreciate them."* The disciple was disheartened. *"There is no alternative"* the master suddenly said, *"you'll have to dive into these oceanic scriptures, navigate yourself to the depths, and find those priceless jewels for yourself."* The disciple understood. No shortcuts, cheap bargains or quick gains. If you want jewels, you have to put in the effort to mine them.

So maybe it's the answer you didn't want, but you'll have to find the top five verses for yourself. Krishna wants to have that conversation with you.

Can you explain Karma more clearly?

The terminology is more complex than people think. *Karma* can refer to multiple things. *Karma* literally means an action. But *karma* can also refer to a reaction that appears after an action is performed. Most commonly, *karma* refers to the law which governs what reactions are dispensed as per someone's actions.

The purpose of *karma* is educational - like a parent rewarding or punishing a child. Behind it all is love, expressed in different ways according to what the child needs to improve. So, *karma* is a universal system of education created by a loving God, aimed to help us elevate our consciousness. In the Bhagavad-gita and various other writings, we find the science of *karma* described, explaining what kind of actions trigger various reactions. The basic idea is that good activities generate good reactions – if you offer charity in this life, for example, then in the next life you'll get that money back manifold. Krishna also describes vikarma, destructive and harmful actions, which bring reactions of pain and suffering, aimed at reforming us so we interact with others and the world in a different way.

Beyond the good and bad of this world, however, the law of *karma* is meant to usher us towards spiritual activity, also known as *akarma*. These kinds of activities take us beyond material duality and the complexities of entanglement, guiding us to the spiritual realm where we live unbound and free.

How does Karma affect me?

If we broadly look at our life, then we can see a stage is built for us. Our previous actions have a bearing on four major things in this life.

We have a certain upbringing and family situation; this is known as *janma*. We are each endowed with a certain amount of opulence, wealth and material prosperity; this is known as *aisvarya*. Each of us have a certain cognitive, intellectual and analytical capacity; this is known as *sruta*. And finally, we all look a certain way - physical beauty and attractiveness; known as *sri*. These are all the effects of previous actions playing out in this life as karmic reactions. How we act upon this 'karmic stage' will determine our next situation.

I struggle to see that everything is good – some things just seem bad!

Sometimes we can become so philosophical that we become unreal! I don't think we have to force ourselves to see everything as good - but we can say that something good can come from everything that happens. There is a difference. Nobody deserves to suffer and we wouldn't wish bad *karma* upon anyone. When we step away, however, and resist the

temptation to constantly judge everything in the moment, we can find
bigger takeaways.

In order to understand the depth of *karma* we first have to appreciate
the length and breadth of our existence. Firstly, the length of our
existence is longer than we think – this life is just one chapter, the
events and experiences are part of a bigger masterplan on our journey
of life. Secondly, the breadth of our life is broader than we think – we are
not just material bodies and minds, but spiritual souls. Thus, *karma*,
even when painful for the body and mind, can awaken something on a
spiritual level that brings us closer to our original pure consciousness.

Can too much spiritual knowledge be bad?

There's two ways you can get blinded. Firstly, when there's no light at all
and secondly when there is too much light! Have you ever tried looking
into the sun? Everything ends up blurry! There is something to learn
from this. If you don't have any wisdom in your life you are blinded,
but if you have an overload of information without contextualising,
digesting and applying, you may remain blinded. If you don't embed
that information in a deep space within your consciousness, you can
actually drown in it.

That's exactly why I emphasise 'wisdom that breathes' – we are not here
just to be repositories of information, where we memorise lots of facts
and figures and stories, accounts and passages of scripture. We have to
deeply absorb that wisdom, observe it playing out around us, apply it
in our lives and the way we function. We have to let that wisdom touch
our heart and transform our consciousness. We have to see Divinity
speaking to us through that wisdom.

When we interact with wisdom in that way then we'll never be overloaded and it will always feel nourishing to the heart. The purpose of studying this deep wisdom is not to *know* God, but rather to *love* God. We are not in the business of trying to know the entirety of Divinity, but we're in the business of trying to become captured in heart, mind and soul in a beautiful relationship with Divinity. Wisdom must be couched within a very reflective, sincere spiritual heart that tries to bring it alive. Otherwise, it can just feel very intellectual and dry and make you proud and insensitive. Knowledge can be misused and misapplied.

Our monastery is known as Bhaktivedanta Manor. When new people come, I ask them: *"are you a person of the head or the heart?"* They all give different answers. I tell them that *bhakti* means devotion (the heart) and *vedanta* means knowledge (the head) – so the Bhaktivedanta Manor is where the head and heart meet.

How does cyclical time work?

In Judeo-Christian traditions time is depicted in a linear fashion where there's a beginning and an end. In the Vedic scheme, however, the notion is that time progresses in a cyclical fashion. You could liken it to seasons. Just like we have winter, spring, summer and autumn, so in the universal cycle there are four cosmic seasons, or what we call *yugas* (ages). The current age, known as *kali-yuga*, is considered the dark age, the most degraded and troubled time in cosmic history.

Scriptures explain that God descends in all four seasons to ignite spiritual resurgence. Such divine appearances are known as *avatars*, which literally means 'to cross down.' In English we say incarnation.

The current Kali-yuga commenced 5,000 years ago and was initiated on the day that Krishna left the world. Since then, there has been a steady decline in the overall prosperity and wellbeing of society. 500 years ago, Krishna again descended to the world, this time in the identity of Sri Chaitanya and popularised the means of spiritual elevation in these troubled times. That path of perfection is founded upon the chanting of God's Holy Name.

Why is Krishna so different from our normal conception of God?

Some think of God as a strict and unforgiving judge; the old man who sits on a grand throne and hurls down thunderbolts every time someone deviates. Others consider Him a crutch for the weak, an imaginary being who brings peace, hope and comfort, but has little to do with objective reality. Still others think of God as a mythological tool of the power-hungry elite, used to keep the masses in line and maintain the status quo. For many, God is simply the cosmic order-supplier; a convenient port of call in times of need and want.

The Vedic literature paints a dramatically different picture. Their extraordinary revelation is not only that God exists, but that He is bursting with colour, character and bliss. God is *'raso vai sah'* – the complete embodiment of affectionate relationships and irresistible sweetness.

Fredrick Nietzsche once said, *"I would only believe in a God that knows how to dance!"*

Lord Krishna, the Supreme Personality, eternally resides in the spiritual world. That realm is known as Vrindavana, the place of no anxiety, the place where every step is a dance, every word a song and where all relationships are infused with selfless love. It's the playground of God. In that abode the spontaneous and natural relationships with

Krishna transcend rituals, formalities and reverences, fully satisfying the heart's yearning. Song and dance, the two most powerful forms of emotional expression, are integral parts of the daily schedule.

Maybe Nietszche was searching for Krishna, the enchanting fluteplayer who dances with the cowherd maidens in the moonlight. Maybe we all are. More than His greatness, His incredible sweetness is what captures the heart of His devotees.

How can we be sure that our connection to Krishna isn't just a concoction of the mind?

Is spirituality a self-fulfilling prophecy? In other words, you believe Krishna exists, you want to see Krishna, therefore you project in your mind that you are seeing Krishna, when actually there may not be much substance to it!

First and foremost, to be fair, we'd have to table the same scepticism against everything else of this world. The media tells you that buying a fast car will make you happy, you work hard to get it and when you do you convince yourself it makes you happy. How many of the material successes and so-called fulfilling achievements of this world are self-fulfilling prophecies, brainwashed into our psyche through the weapons of mass instruction like the media and entertainment powerhouses?

In Krishna Consciousness, the experience of Divinity and feelings of connection with Krishna are surely personal ones. But we can also see very objective measures of that experience in terms of tangible transformation. When one experiences Divinity, their character improves and they elevate themselves to a significantly higher level of saintliness and selflessness. They also become averse to destructive desires and ways of living that harm themselves, others and the world in general. One who experiences Divinity becomes detached from everything that the world is running after, something which can only really be possible if they are experiencing a positive alternative, some higher taste.

Though the experience of Divinity is an internal feeling, it also reflects in dramatic external changes. Furthermore, there is a deep and complex theology and spiritual science behind it which explains and unpacks this transformation.

You worship Krishna so opulently – wouldn't He be happier if you fed the poor with that money instead?

These are natural questions. *Why spend so much money on flowers, dresses and golden ornaments for elaborate temple worship? Wouldn't God be happier if we spent that money on helping the poverty stricken? Is God pleased when we offer Him sumptuous feasts while thousands of malnourished individuals lie on the temple doorstep? Are we satisfied in building huge, ornate marble temples while orphaned children suffer in makeshift shanty towns? Have we become so interested in our own spiritual wellbeing that we've lost touch with the 'real' world?*

These acts of worship are not simply token, mechanical deeds, but thoughtful activities meant to invoke a sense of awareness and personal relationship with God. While we are impersonal and insensitive toward the Divine, it is very difficult to be personal and sensitive toward the multitude of living beings around us. Scriptures do state that one who simply performs ritual worship but does not work to alleviate the sufferings of others is a neophyte and elementary practitioner. However, that does not deem ritual worship void. Performed in the proper spirit, such rituals invoke a deep spiritual vision, where one becomes sensitive to everything in the universe, seeing different creations as part of the Divine. On that level, the spiritualist feels the sufferings of others as his own suffering and dedicates their life for spiritual upliftment.

So yes, spiritualists should help the world in tangible ways. Their more unique contribution, however, is to help people develop genuine spirituality and the vision of equality. These spiritual individuals can trigger change on a deeper level.

Does the Bhagavad-gita promote violence and religious war?

In ancient Vedic scriptures we find the famous aphorism, *ahimsyat sarva bhutanam* – *"one should not commit violence to any living being."* Since nonviolence is a cardinal principle of the spiritualists, they are urged to refrain from causing harm to even animals or plants. However, non-violence can mean different things in different situations. As a guardian of the people, the warrior Arjuna was required to take responsibility for the preservation of law and order in society. In this case, his non-violence had to be expressed through confrontational means.

Such strong action is neither taken whimsically, nor for the sake of material gain and never with a mood of hatred or envy. It was the last resort and even when the battle commenced, it was fought between consenting parties who followed strict moral and ethical codes of conduct. Before drawing any parallels between the Battle of Kurukshetra and modern warfare, one must look into the historical, moral and social context of each circumstance.

History shows that violence has touched every part of the world, independent of the theological beliefs of people. In fact, the most destructive wars, were fought for secular, political, economic, or ideological reasons. Religion is not the cause of conflict – on the contrary, it is the very neglect of genuine spirituality that causes war, violence and unrest in this world. Societies of genuine spiritualists hold great reverence for life. Qualities of respect, contentment, humility and tolerance are the cornerstones of their existence.

Saints who have delivered the Bhagavad-gita to the modern world have affirmed that the real revolution in society is to transform people's hearts through selflessness and love. The real revolution is one of of consciousness. To solve the problem of violence, the answer is not to reject spirituality, but rather to restore and revive it in its true nature and spirit.

Why do you worship idols?

In dialogues with those from Judeo-Christian or Islamic backgrounds, I regularly encounter some uneasiness as to how God can appear in a 'material' form – idols made by the hands of man. It appears limiting, imaginary and almost childish to treat God like a play-doll by dressing Him, feeding Him and putting Him to bed at night. Can God truly reveal His divine self through material elements? Can a factual and deep relationship with God be established via such rituals?

While many see the material world as completely separate from the Supreme Spirit, the ancient Vedic tradition defines God as the source of everything material and spiritual (*janmadya asya yatah*). Even physical elements have an intimate relationship with God. The cause is present in the effect. Thus, God's imminence in the material world may be brought to the surface when material objects, such as marble, metal or wood, are directly engaged as vehicles of worship according to authorised prescriptions. God, after all, is the 'complete whole' and can simultaneously manifest Himself in everything within and beyond our experience. To say He cannot appear in a certain way would be to place a limitation on the Supreme.

How do you view death?

As a young monk, I remember enthusiastically volunteering to attend funerals whenever the opportunity arose. For me they were a reality check, a confirmation and an impetus to dig deeper. Even today, sages in the East cover themselves in ashes and meditate in front of flower-decked funeral pyres as a means to bolster their spiritual urgency. Steve Jobs appreciated that death was life's most effective change-agent. While addressing thousands of Stamford graduates, he commented: *"remembering that you are going to die is the best way I know to avoid the trap of thinking you have something to lose. You are already naked. There is no reason not to follow your heart."*

Yet we do indeed avoid it, living in a society where death is sterilised, sanitised and carefully sealed off from public view. They say 72% of people die without writing a will. Maybe they thought it would never happen to them. Maybe they just didn't want to think about it. Despite our resistance and defiance, time and tide wait for no man.

Death, however, need not be seen as an inconvenient truth but rather the ultimate meditation to reinstate clarity and perspective into every aspect of our life. Death reminds us of our priorities – those critical things we have to pursue before time runs out. Death brings gratitude. Through the lens of temporality, we perceive everything and everyone we complain about in a new light. Death counters laziness. No point in killing time once you realise that time is actually killing you. Death

brings fearlessness. In the face of permanent expiry, all of our worries   **179**
and anxieties pale in into insignificance.

RAPID FIRE

Over the years interviewers have often asked me questions which were meant to be entertaining and engaging for the audience, with the added benefit of bringing a personal insight into the 'face behind the words.' Those questions actually helped me to learn more about myself and my journey in life - when we look back and introspect we can often see connections and find lessons. Here I reproduce some of those 'rapid-fire' questions and my intuitive answers.

What was your favourite subject at school?

My highest grades were always in Maths and it's where I excelled. I've been given a type of mathematical intelligence that naturally detects patterns, organises things into structures, quantifies objects and creates formulas that can help decode the past and future. I like looking at things systematically and creating order. You may have noticed how this is reflected in my writing, speaking and style of presentation.

Over time, however, I've realised that while there are patterns in the world, there is also personality. Everyone is an individual and sentient. Applying wisdom in the world and our lives isn't a simple copy and paste exercise. Although there are universal spiritual principles, the application and detail of how it relates to a particular person is nuanced. It requires sensitive thinking and lots of compassion and kindness. Nowadays, I try to factor that into my mathematical approach to life so I can serve people better and avoid de-personalising them. Formulas are a good starting point, but then we need to add in a bit of heart.

What do you do first thing in the morning?

In monastic training, one of the first things we were taught is to bow down as soon as you wake up. It's a beautiful culture which has become part of me. In colloquial English we often say *"you have to become grounded,"* or, *"stop living with your head in the clouds."* There is a sense in which bowing our head to the ground brings us back to reality and nurtures a clarity of consciousness.

When we bow down we reestablish the humble identity of being a servant in this world. When we bow down we pray for forgiveness and also the ability to forgive. When we bow down we offer our prayers and gratitude for everything we have received from others. When we

bow down, it engenders a meekness which brings us closer to Divinity.
If we are constantly looking down on others, we will never be able to
see God and all his miracles above us. Thus, when the sun rises the first
thing we do is bow down.

What's the last thing you do before sleeping?

In my sleeping bag I do a mental re-run of the whole day. I rewind
to the moment I woke up and review the activities, interactions and
experiences of the day. My main purpose is to see how well I utilised
my time, whether there were missed opportunities and how I could
have been more effective. On most days, I fall asleep before the analysis
is complete, which is usually a good sign!

One of the cardinal principles I've always tried to follow is to
religiously avoid time-wasting. In today's world most people complain
about not having enough time, but my experience has revealed two
very powerful things. Firstly, when time is properly utilised, then
time actually expands. Divinity reciprocates with your diligence
by magically opening up windows of time so that you can do more.
Secondly, when desire deepens, capacity increases. When we can't
bear to waste any time because we have so many important things to
achieve, it activates a divine empowerment which allows you to do
more in the same amount of time. Activities which would normally
consume large amounts of time are completed much quicker. Because
of these two factors, you see how highly motivated spiritual people
can achieve colossal things in a seemingly limited amount of time.

What would you change about yourself?

One mentor once joked with me saying, *"tall people live in towers and it's easy for them to walk around all day and look down on others."* Later, I realised it was more than a joke. When I reflect on my interactions, one of the things I've discovered is my annoying tendency to judge others and project myself onto them. We all have our God-given capacities, abilities and personalities, and it's so easy to view everyone through that lens. I expect people to approach and live life as I do and when they don't, I hold that against them.

This is something I am trying to rectify. When we judge others, we don't improve, the person doesn't improve and the relationship doesn't improve. I'm learning to stop making judgements unless it's absolutely necessary. If I do, I try to communicate with and understand the person before I come to a conclusion. Even then, I'm open to the fact that I could be wrong. I also try to remember the famous quote by Goethe: *"Treat a man as he is and he will remain as he is. But treat him as he can and should be and he will become what he can and should be."*

What is your life mission?

I've identified what has been most transformational in my life and naturally feel like that's what I should be sharing with the world. Thus, sharing 'wisdom that breathes' has become my full-time occupation (and obsession!). It's incredibly rewarding to see how discussing this wisdom changes people's lives, gives them hope, creates spiritual vision and empowers them to overcome obstacles and difficulties.

It is, however, an iterative process. I try to *read* the wisdom, *contemplate* the wisdom, *live* the wisdom and then *share* that wisdom.

That cycle continues perpetually, as we spiral to unlimited depths.
Sharing wisdom without doing the prior steps just doesn't work. So I
guess my life mission is to simultaneously be an eternal student and
teacher because I think those two identities are inseparable and also
dynamically connected.

What's your favourite colour?

It would have to be orange and more specifically, saffron. Of course,
it's traditionally the colour of the renunciates, but that's not the reason
since I don't see renunciation as the goal of life. What saffron stands
for, however, is deep and extremely meaningful.

Saffron represents fire and, in the spiritual context, the complete
incineration of material desires and attachments. This annihilation
of all material attachment opens up the head-space and heart-space
to cultivate real love and devotion. Alongside the burning of the
external, saffron also represents the burning heart – that intense
desire to connect with the Supreme Person and the ultimate reality.
There is perhaps no more graphic imagery of intensity than a burning
fire. Wearing saffron cloth reminds us of how that inner intensity will
define our progress on the spiritual journey.

What's a good piece of advice you received?

When I was struggling to keep up with the early morning routine at
the temple, a mentor told me, *"When the alarm clock goes off, get up,
dress up and show up – this is the most important work in the world!"*
It may sound a little harsh, almost like a boot camp instruction which
lacks heart, but I have to say it has helped me hugely over the years.

Spirituality is about experience, taste, inspiration and feeling. But another major aspect is too often neglected – discipline, duty and determination. There is much to be said about 'getting on with it,' despite how we feel in the moment. If we could fortify this unglamorous aspect of our spiritual life we could grow to unimaginable heights. The vows of the great saints were like lines in stone; once uttered, there was no question of retraction. Their vows were planted in the heart and watered for many years, eventually producing wonderfully sweet fruits. Although somewhat bitter to digest, I now treasure this advice and I often remember it first thing in the morning!

What is your happiest memory in life?

When we think of the happiest memory, it's generally a highlight – an achievement, unique experience, unexpected fortune or break from the norm. For me, however, it's quite the opposite!

Over a decade ago, I began visiting Vrindavana, the holy pilgrimage town, for one month every year. I would travel alone, or perhaps with one person and for the most part go 'off the grid.' We would live simply, eat simply, and follow the same daily routine, which would incorporate the same activities. There were no surprises or special treats, but just the same spiritual routine, every single day. In this, I experienced a completely different type of happiness. It felt so non-pretentious. A simple, sustainable and spiritual type of happiness which was based on something beyond the external conditions. Finding happiness in nothing that outwardly special, taught me that simple spirituality was the most special thing in the world.

I have a transcendental job! I read somewhere that I should *"make my day-dream my day-job."* That's what I've tried to do in my life. I reflected on this in a homage to Srila Prabhupada I wrote recently:

"Srila Prabhupada, you're my boss, the business of Chaitanya-deva has become my occupation and the salary is the gradual awakening of divine love. My colleagues are the saintly, over-time is a pleasure, holidays are unnecessary and the retirement plan is out of this world. May I be more determined and driven than the people out there chasing a million bucks. May I ready myself for more sacrifices than the city sharks who'll 'go to hell and back' to conquer the corporate ladder. May I happily embrace more risks than those willing to jeopardise everything to realise their greedy ambitions."

Whose death hit you the hardest?

In recent years many dear friends and mentors have departed the world, but I guess the one that hit me the hardest was my fellow monk, Janakinath (aka JD), who passed away in 2022. In the book *'Loving Life, Embracing Death'* I write of the many lessons I learnt from the time we spent together.

JD was 'one of us.' He wasn't a celebrity devotee, a distinguished pioneer, a veteran of the movement, a leader with a title or someone possessing extraordinary abilities. Internally, however, he had developed a purity that is rarely observed. In the face of unimaginable provocation and challenge, he displayed a unique level of spiritual equipoise that the ancient scriptures portray and revere as symptomatic of perfection. His departure was particularly difficult, because it revealed to me how much I underestimate and take for granted those around me.

How do you cope with hardship?

If you ever see an ECG, then it constantly flows through peaks and troughs. A flat line signifies death. In the same way, life means ups and downs, and dealing with hardships, challenges, obstacles and let-downs is therefore one of the most prized of skills in the human repertoire.

For a good period of my life, I got into the habit of rising by 3.00am every morning. The temple community would congregationally gather at 4.30am, so that gave me one hour of solitude in the stillness of the early morning to deeply connect with the eternal reality. I've always seen that making that kind of investment in uplifting the consciousness through wisdom lends you an immunity to the chaos of this world. It's like launching yourself into the spiritual skies and activating the vision of eternity. On that backdrop, the obstacles and difficulties of life shrink in their significance.

What motivates you the most in your journey?

I feel the biggest difference between spirituality and religion is that one triggers deep transformation, while the other remains cultural and largely ritualistic. When I see the process of spirituality creating significant change in myself and others it gives me a deep motivation to venture further. It's amazing how your vision, goals, desires and character changes by disciplined application. It's wonderful to see how the indicators of progress predicted in the scripture can be observed in real life. You tangibly experience that this is wisdom that breathes – it works!

I've experienced how spirituality can transform people in the most dramatic and also sustainable ways. It's so hope-giving because I think many have surrendered to the idea that they are who they are. Many have given up on changing themselves, feeling it to be impossible, impractical and unattainable. The spiritual process works on such a deep level that it can overcome these internal blocks that we encounter.

What was the most pivotal relationship in your life?

Perhaps many of us would say this, but definitely my parents built the foundation for my life. Although my spiritual inspirers, mentors and gurus were the ones who moulded my life, I felt they were able to do that because my parents had made me 'fertile.' The values, the sensitivity, the culture, all meant that when the spiritual wisdom did land in my heart, I was primed to accept it, apply it and take greater advantage.

Later, when I decided to adopt monastic life, it was my parents who became the biggest opposition. In hindsight, I see how their opposition was actually a great gift. It helped me become more resolute, more sincere, more focused and deeply thoughtful about what I was doing. It meant that when I did enter monastic life, I didn't take it for granted and fall into familiarity or complacency. Their reservation made me work for that opportunity and it made me take everything much more seriously.

What trait most defines who you are?

You'd have to ask that to others! There is, however, a verse from the scriptures that I hold in high esteem and which has become a guiding light and 'north star' in my life. The teachers recommend we wear this verse around our neck at all times. They say that our advancement in spirituality will be proportionate to how much we imbibe the principles of this verse in our life. When Srila Prabhupada was asked what made him such an advanced devotee, he smiled and humbly said *"I have the formula for that medicine, but I havent been able to produce it yet!"* The formula he was referrring to, was this very same verse:

"One should chant the holy name of the Lord in a humble state of mind, thinking oneself lower than the straw in the street; one should be more tolerant than a tree, devoid of all sense of false prestige and should be ready to offer all respect to others. In such a state of mind one can chant the holy name of the Lord constantly." (Sri Siksastakam Verse 3, Chaitanya Mahaprabhu)

What is your most strongly held belief?

There are many aspects of the spiritual reality which, though they make sense, are somewhat beyond my grasp at this point in time. One thing I do have deep faith in, however, is the purity, character and spiritual standing of Srila Prabhupada, the inspiration behind the movement. His clarity, conviction, courage and compassion remain the guiding beacon in my life.

We are all human and I think it's natural for everyone to experience times of weakness and compromise. In him, however, I see a level of spiritual consistency that is rarely observed. His sustained spiritual enthusiasm over the entirety of his life, his chastity and loyalty to his principles, his willingness to undergo personal discomfort for the benefit of others, his level of faith and conviction in navigating his mission - all of this indicates a deep level of spiritual purity and connection. Even when aspects of his character and presentation have been difficult to understand, I've been able to face that challenge and grasp deeper truths.

What stranger do you still think about sometimes?

Once, I was in a town called Kettering, meeting people on the high street and sharing books of wisdom. Early in the day an old lady came to me, fascinated by what I was doing. I explained to her how I had graduated from university but had opted to become a monk and now spent my days sharing spirituality with anyone and everyone. She was moved by that and clearly very appreciative. As a Christian, her strong conviction was that I had all the ingredients for spiritual success, an ideal candidate, but that I should adopt the Christian path. She wasn't pushy, preachy or judgemental, but genuinely believed in her path and wished the best for me. We cordially parted after some time.

About thirty minutes later I spotted her on the benches watching me. She sat there for the next five hours without budging. As I finished for the day and began walking back to the car park, she came running behind me. With tears in her eyes she said she had been intently waiting to speak to me – for over five hours! I was shocked by her patience! She had gone to Waterstones, bought a beautiful copy of the Bible, written a heart-warming message in it and said she was eagerly waiting to gift it to me. She did it with such love and kindness. It was genuine and truly heartfelt.

I reflected on whether I had spoken to anyone that day with the same level of kindness and genuine care. Without saying it in these terms, she reminded me – *"it's one thing to love to preach, but quite another to love the people you preach to!"*

What is your deepest fear?

I have lived a very active and energetic life. A deep-rooted fear is what will happen when I lose that capacity. In recent years I have witnessed the journey of three cancer patients from their diagnosis to their final days, observing how gradually everything was taken away from them. They were all more active and energetic than me, but in due course of time, they were stripped of their physical vitality, cognitive abilities, freedom of movement and became forcibly dependent on others. Through that deterioration, however, they maintained an incredible level of grace and resilience and their hunger and enthusiasm for life never waned.

They were able to do that because of spiritual immersion. When everything externally shuts down, the only other place we have to live is the internal world. If we haven't developed that spiritual connection, however, we'll feel frustrated, limited and severely impaired in our life when such challenges come. It's a constant reminder for me to invest in that deep spiritual consciousness, knowing that one day, everything material and external will inevitably fade away. It's only a matter of time.

What do you think people misunderstand about you?

In recent years my life has become more and more public and I think people perceive me as a confident, outgoing and sociable person. They see me as a leader and someone who comfortably stands at the front and takes charge. People may classify me as an extrovert more than an introvert. They think that when I'm in front of an audience or a camera then I'm 'in my element.' In reality, however, it's quite the opposite!

By nature I am introverted, shy and reserved. I get energy when I'm in solitude or in quiet, reflective spaces. For the purpose of serving the world, however, I've trained myself in public speaking, leading, managing and social life. I guess the desire to serve helps you overcome personal inhibitions and limitations and embrace that which would normally be totally alien. To this day I feel nervous when in front of an auidence and would happily let someone else take the lead if they could do the same job. That said, although it's uncomfortable, the satisfaction of being able to serve others carries me through and gives a wonderful feeling.

What makes you angry?

I find exploitation really hard to stomach. When I see the rich manipulate the poor, the powerful use their influence to control the weak, the knowledgeable harness their capacity to control and subjugate others, then I feel the need to act and speak out. In spiritual circles, we're taught to use our abilities, facilities and identities to serve others and assist them in becoming happier, healthier and wiser.

In the material world, however, people use what they have to take advantage of others. Thus, we see so many problems in the world today, including breakdowns of relationships, communities and genuine love between human beings.

What is humanity's worst quality?

The fundamental problem is that humanity is based upon a lie. This lie is so widespread that it has permeated practically every culture around the world and has perpetuated for generations. This lie is accepted even by people who claim they don't and it's the lie which creates the greatest number of subsequent lies. This lie, though exposed again and again, still keeps living. It's a lie which imprisons us in a way of living that blocks us from real happiness.

The biggest lie in the world is that material achievements, material success, material objects, material relationships, material situations and material arrangements will make you happy. And if you look at every other lie that's there in the world, it's a lie that facilitates this lie or is based upon this lie.

What is a lesson that took you a long time to learn?

I'm still trying to learn the golden lesson that 'honesty is the best policy.' According to the cosmic cycle described in the Vedas, we are living in the most corrupted epoch. Four fundamental principles underpin any functional society, organization, family or group; self-control, cleanliness, compassion and truthfulness. When individuals wholeheartedly embrace these virtues, success is guaranteed on every level – physically, emotionally, socially and most importantly, spiritually. The analysis of the sages however, reveals that today, three of the four are practically obliterated and society now delicately hinges on the single principle of truthfulness. The irony – to conceal our frail character and avoid exposing those predictable deficiencies, we end up fabricating lies, lies and more lies! The tendency towards deceit and dishonesty then, is the proverbial nail in the coffin.

One of the biggest criteria for deepening our spirituality is the strength to be open and honest. Instead, however, we are often closed and pretentious. In the name of saving our face, we kill our soul. Sometimes we invent, sometimes we withhold, sometimes we exaggerate and sometimes we stay quiet and let the lies roll – a variety of ingenious ways in which we compromise our integrity. Thus, I constantly remind myself that weakness is not a disqualification, but dishonesty and lying surely creates a spiritual block.

What do you hope to accomplish in 10 years?

I have always tried to view life inside out. If I can change the ecology of my own heart, then I feel the doors open up to make a beautiful contribution in the world. Thus, I hope that ten years from now I'll be more spiritually connected, develop greater purity, embody better character and qualities, and have a deeper desire to genuinely serve others out of compassion.

I'm convinced that the spiritual wisdom and tools we have at our disposal can trigger the most profound changes in people and society at large. I'm also convinced that this spiritual wisdom can and will be shared on an unimaginable scale. It's just a matter of time! The only question is whether I will qualify myself to become an instrument in that magical proliferation of wisdom that breathes.

The post-modern mind often rebels against authority figures and the principle of gurus. That approach is more fraternal than hierarchical – position and titles don't mean as much as friendship and kindness. The post-modern are explorative more than definitive – the truth they say, is something we are constantly discovering and absoluteness smells suspicious. Post-modernism promotes inclusivity over exclusivity – nobody has a monopoly, claim or control over the truth, they say. Though these notions may sound antithetical to traditional spirituality and the acceptance of a guru, not necessarily.

In Vedic tradition, the guru is as much a loving friend as a protective father, eagerly waiting to give independence and empowerment so that the disciple can creatively design their destiny. The guru lends vision and opens doors, allowing the disciple to explore a previously inaccessible world of opportunity. The guru teaches the absolute truth, but then encourages the disciple to mine that oceanic knowledge for their own jewels of wisdom and insight. The relationship with gurus and guides is one of the most mystical and beautiful components of the spiritual journey. In this section, I share my appreciation for the two most prominent teachers in my life.

GURU &
GUIDES
Words of Gratitude

SRILA PRABHUPADA

The Sanskrit word for gratitude is krta-jna, which literally means "to know what has been done for you." In the life of a spiritualist there are periodic times in the day when we pause for gratitude – when we wake up, when we go to bed, when we eat, when we commence spiritual discussion, when we have a success or failure... the spiritualists even pause at sunrise, zenith and sunset for a prayer of gratitude. Since gratitude is said to be the mother of all qualities, by deeply nourishing that disposition within us, all good things naturally follow.

One personality who I feel immensely grateful towards is Srila Prabhupada, formally known as A.C. Bhaktivedanta Swami. Behind his colossal achievements and ground-breaking contributions is a magnetic spiritual character and personality that continues to capture my imagination even today. Every year on his 'appearance day,' or birthday, we take some moments to offer some heartfelt words of appreciation.

INTENSIVE CARE (JAN 2018)

Dear Srila Prabhupada,

Please accept my humble obeisances. All glories to your divine grace!

Today I'm remembering your incredible sacrifices, unending compassion and resolute determination. You tried everything, went everywhere and approached everyone, leaving no stone unturned in your mission to uplift as many souls as possible. You were deeply concerned, meditating on your mission at every moment, tirelessly planning and plotting for a revolution of consciousness.

If I'm bold enough to call myself your follower, if I'm genuinely grateful for what you've given me, how can I not embody the same acute care and concern for furthering your missionary work in this world? Though trying to avoid the egotistical desire to 'make my mark,' I'm impelled to share the 'fruits' I've received from you as far and wide as possible. It's clear, however, that I am falling short.

Projects have come and gone, ideas have worked and then fallen apart, and some initiatives were thriving and then slowed down. What will I really have to offer you after all is said and done? Everything I'm trying is a 'work-in-progress' and slow progress at that. I'm sorry I don't have something more substantial to report.

Recently I've been attempting to hone in on what is actually required to build strong, sustainable, successful, spiritual projects. My conclusion: intensive care. If we don't intensively care about what we do, in no time those projects will end up in the ICU, nearing death. I'm asking myself the hard question: *how much do I deeply, genuinely and sincerely care about my services in your movement?* To deeply care about something means:

- To never give up.

- To be ready and willing to do whatever it takes.
- To give quality time and undivided attention.
- To be constantly meditating on the goal.
- To maintain enthusiasm, despite an absence of results and reciprocation.
- To invest all physical and mental capacities.
- To harbour no hidden agendas or personal motivations.
- To go that 'extra mile' that nobody else would consider.
- To be so immersed in the goal, that 'getting the credit' pales into insignificance.

You exuded all these qualities, never waning in dedication to your own Guru. On the order of Bhaktisiddhanta Saraswati Thakur, you shed 200 gallons of blood to spread this movement across the globe. Please bless me so I can develop an ounce of that deep care and concern for serving this mission – for me, it seems the most fitting way to express my insignificant *"thank you"* for everything you have given me.

Begging to remain, in your transcendental service,

Sutapa das

BEING CHALLENGED (AUG 2019)

Dear Srila Prabhupada,

Please accept my humble obeisances. All glories to you!

Your life is a challenge.

I'm challenged to overcome my weakness. You were savagely attacked from all sides – critical journalists, irate parents, deviant followers, fault-finding contemporaries. A barrage of negativity directed towards a selfless saint who only desired the greatest good for everyone. The dogs may bark but the caravan moves on – unfazed and undeterred, you marched forward. You taught us what determination is.

I'm challenged to overcome my selfishness. From morning to night, day after day, in every imaginable forum, you were teaching, writing, serving, counselling, encouraging and problem solving. Using every last bit of energy and every single drop of blood, to further the vision of Srila Bhaktisiddhanta Saraswati. You taught us what it means to be completely selfless.

I'm challenged to overcome my hard-heartedness. Though a heavy-duty general in a missionary movement, you humoured the children, personally cared for sick devotees, constantly prayed for the wellbeing of your disciples and cried when you saw street kids rummaging in the rubbish heap for leftover scraps of food. The courage of an English soldier and the love of a Bengali mother. You taught us how Vaisnavas have a heart.

I'm challenged to overcome my shallowness. You gazed at the Deities through eyes salved with love, genuine teardrops fell when you sang Krishna names and your beseeching speech, infused with a heavyweight dose of compassion, penetrated people's hearts. The depth of your devotion defied human limits. You taught us to reside close to Krishna at every single moment.

Your life is a constant challenge to think bigger, dive deeper, extend further and become stronger. I'm begging for a bit more time to get my act together so I can offer you something worthwhile. Ideas are there, but I'm lacking the purity and transcendental intelligence to manifest them. By your mercy, we live to fight another day. Fallen but hopeful, I'm expecting your mercy so I can offer some worthwhile service, insignificant as I am.

I beg to remain, in your transcendental service,

Sutapa das

POWERHOUSE OF LOVE (AUG 2020)

Dear Srila Prabhupada,

Please accept my humble obeisances. All glories to you!

There are many poetic ways to describe love. One great saint, whose writings you revered and repeatedly referenced, penned this beautiful insight:

"When the affectionate bond between a young man and a young woman can never be destroyed, even when there is every cause for the destruction of that relationship, the attachment between them is said to be pure love." This is the nature of the eternal loving affairs between Lord Krishna and His pure associates. (Visvanatha Cakravarti Thakur)

Even the most acute challenges cannot jeopardise the relationship of lovers. Nothing can impede the divine flow of loving service exchanged between them. You, Srila Prabhupada, are the living proof. Despite unthinkable adversities, your devotion came shining through with increased intensity every single time. You emerged from disturbing situations completely unscathed and ever inspired in your loving offering to Krishna. Unstoppable.

Can we keep going, keep giving, keep serving... even when people frustrate us, disappoint us, ridicule and criticise us in unkind ways, showing an astounding lack of appreciation and gratitude? You did.

Can we keep going, keep giving, keep serving... even when there are reversals, obstacles and intimidating complications which seem insurmountable and thoroughly deflating? You did.

Can we keep going, keep giving, keep serving... even when Krishna's reciprocation isn't immediately apparent and when baffling events start transpiring contrary to our hopes and expectations? You did.

Can we keep going, keep giving, keep serving... expending all available energy, even when the body is failing, the health is declining and the vitality is waning? You did.

Your service, sacrifice and surrender are off the scale. You are a luminary of devotion and a powerhouse of love – the irresistible force that smashes through every material barrier imaginable. Your seamless connection with Lord Krishna, mediated by Sri Guru, was entirely uninterrupted. For you, the pain of not serving far outweighed any perceived pain we encounter within service – and therefore, in every situation, however challenging, you couldn't stop serving with love. Giving, giving, giving, right till the last breath.

How can I ever make it, so distant from such purity? Stonehearted and dry, I shudder to think what Krishna must feel like to be on the receiving end of my apathetic offerings. I sometimes wonder if I'll ever get there. But then I smile, knowing that I'm connected to the powerhouse of love. You came to our level, captured our imagination, conquered our hearts and connected us to the most mystical movement in creation. Though I'm a beggar, impoverished in love, your brilliance is drawing out some devotion from my steel-framed heart. Please accept me as a tiny servant in your masterplan to jolt this crazy world out of spiritual amnesia. Please give me a chance to serve you – everything else, quite frankly, is a useless waste of time. When all is said and done, our connection with you will be our saving grace.

Begging to remain, close to your lotus feet,

Sutapa das

KEEP ON MOVING (JAN 2020)

Dear Srila Prabhupada,

Please accept my humble obeisances. All glories to you!

You described your spiritual master as a *"Vaikuntha man,"* and it's blatantly obvious that you were no different. More specifically, a *"Vrindavana man"* who travelled to the end of Earth and back, shedding gallons of blood to tell the world about Krishna. *Vraja* literally means *"to move."* The true residents of that holy place are ready and willing to go, do and embrace whatever is required to fulfil Krishna's ever-changing desires. How wonderfully you embodied this spirit!

When family life impeded your cherished mission, you walked away without disappointment. When, in a shocking dream, you were summoned to accept *sannyasa (the renounced order of life)*, you moved with the mysterious desires of Sri Guru. When the opportunity arose to journey to America, though penniless, you daringly ventured into the unknown. When preaching prospects arose in the Lower East Side, Skid Row, the rat-ridden 94-Bowery, you relocated without any hesitation whatsoever. You racked up the air miles, leaving no stone unturned, embracing every possible opportunity to share your message. When a disciple explained that he wanted to eternally reside at your lotus feet, *"it will be very difficult,"* you replied, *"because I'm always moving!"* You were a 'mover and shaker' in the deepest sense of the term. No hesitation, no holding back, ready to move with the plan of Krishna. Fearless, flexible and fully available.

Please help me understand your desires. Please help me lock them in the innermost chambers of my heart. Please bless me with Vrindavana consciousness; no hesitation, no holding back, ready to go with the plan of Krishna. Keep on moving. Fearless, flexible and fully available. This time, somehow or other, I have to get it right.

You were Krishna's own man. Lofty and presumptuous as it may sound, may I one day become a 'Prabhupada man.' What else could we wish for?

Begging to remain, in your transcendental service,

Sutapa das

A LIVING ENIGMA (NOV 2020)

Dear Srila Prabhupada,

Thousands of respects to you!

You were the local mendicant, the unassuming resident of Vrindavana, humbly residing at your simple but tranquil quarters at Radha Damodara Temple. Then you travelled to the Lower East Side and lived alongside the bums of the Bowery. People were shocked that you had relocated to the skid row of New York, but in those alien surroundings you were completely at peace. You were always living with Krishna, living with the order of Guru and therefore everywhere was home for you. *Who can understand your consciousness?*

You were a streetwise manager, practical and bold, one step ahead and as sharp as a saw. *"I'm a Calcutta boy"* you told your disciples, *"nobody can cheat me!"* Yet you were simultaneously a complete saint, generous and kind, fanning the spark without calculation and compassionately bringing out the best in others. You were willing to extend yourself beyond the call of duty regardless of mistakes, weakness or fall down of your disciples. *Who can understand your heart?*

You unflinchingly called rich industrialists 'thieves,' learned scientists 'rascals,' and dubious politicians 'demoniac.' Your speech was harder than a thunderbolt. Yet you embodied deep humility, offered all credit to your guru and shed tears of gratitude while thanking your disciples for their sincere endeavours to help. You were also, without doubt, softer than a rose. *Who can understand your character?*

You lived such a public life – thousands of lectures, hours of meetings, one interview after another and endless conversations. You were followed, recorded and videoed around the clock. In the glaring spotlight, and always completely spotless. Yet your internal life was profound beyond comprehension. In the solitude of the morning hours you bathed in the scriptures, availed of the saintly association of our predecessors and connected so deeply with the holy names of Krishna. You were in constant communion with God. *Who can understand your devotion?*

You were grave and serious, chaste and uncompromising. You never fell short of conveying the absolute truth, exposing the material phantasmagoria time and time again. Yet at the same time you knew how to laugh, a sense of humour which had an appreciation for Charlie Chaplin sketches and the amusing tales of Birbal. Full of joy, you showed how to practice spiritual life with a smile. *Who can understand your shining personality?*

The list goes on... forever and ever. The typing stops here, but my mind is still churning the paradoxical facets of your remarkable character.

Where there is substantial service, sacrifice, seriousness and sincerity...

that's where we meet you. The spiritual master lives forever in his instructions and the follower lives with him. I'm praying for the day when I'll wholeheartedly serve you without hesitancy or resistance. No holding back. Then I have the firm conviction you will call me and I will see you... face to face - the perfection of life. *When, oh when?*

Please don't give up on me,

Sutapa das

JOURNEY INTO THE UNKNOWN (AUG 2021)

Dear Srila Prabhupada,

Please accept my humble obeisances.

All glories to you!

At age 12 you climbed the bamboo scaffolding, 300 feet to the top of the Victoria Memorial. When devotees marvelled at your courage you replied: *"I was brave then and I'm still brave now - otherwise how could I have come to your country at 70 years old?"*

Journey into the Unknown

"When I chant Hare Krishna, I feel no fear" you said, and equipped with that internal poise, nothing could faze you. Your life was a perpetual journey into the unknown, ready to go anywhere, at any time, to try anything in pursuance of your mission.

When family life obstructed your spiritual aspirations, you walked away and became a lone mendicant in Vrindavana... a journey into the unknown. When you received multiple dreams to accept *sannyasa*, though horrifying and inconceivable, you walked that path... a journey into the unknown. When there was an opening to venture to Western lands, despite the trepidation of others, you grabbed it... a journey into the unknown. When Butler, a nice American neighbourhood, no longer facilitated your missionary purposes, you ventured into the urban jungle of hedonism, the Big Apple... a journey into the unknown. When Misra's apartment in Uptown NYC proved fruitless, you descended to the depths of the Lower East Side, the skid row, the lowest of the low... a journey into the unknown.

You never looked for comfort or convenience, only for service and the opportunity to share. You never sought security or safety, ever confident in the divine backup of Krishna, your ever best friend. You never hesitated, fuelled by a volcanic desire to share Krishna Bhakti.

O Prabhupada, grace me with one drop of your fearlessness! Help me overcome the anxiety of embarrassment or failure. Immunize me against the disease of conformity which perpetually confines us within ethereal boundaries. Save me from the trenches of mechanical, mediocre and stagnated spirituality. Please open my heart so I can absorb the inspiration of the Vaisnavas and make their words my North Star. Bless me to embody your spirit and marry the mission of Sri Chaitanya Mahaprabhu.

By your divine grace, in my own small way, I'll try to take some risks, be brave and venture beyond the comfort zone. Insignificant as I am, I'll also try to make a journey into the unknown... eagerly anticipating the prospect of meeting you on the other side.

Yours eternally,

Sutapa das

Dear Srila Prabhupada,

Please accept my humble obeisances. All glories to your divine grace!

Every day we marvel at your colossal achievements, inexplicable through mundane commentary and logic. Today, however, I'm reflecting on the invisible acts of love and devotion that underpinned the spiritual revolution that you instigated – those times of divine communion which nobody saw. It was the blazing fire of pure devotion hidden within you that powerfully set the world alight. How fascinating is the inner life of a pure devotee!

Struggling in the Delhi heat, crying alone in the wilderness, desperately trying to carve out a plan to fulfill the order of your spiritual master. Nobody was listening, success was sparse and how exactly Krishna's will would manifest was unclear, yet you continued on as a lone ranger, waiting for the sweet Lord to intervene and reveal His master plan. Nobody saw that struggle.

The lone mendicant in Vrindavana, sweeping the courtyard of the Radha Damodara temple, praying, petitioning and pleading for mercy. The unknown holy man who sat inconspicuously at the back of the Santipur Temple praying for the blessings of Advaita Acarya. You were positioning yourself to become a divinely empowered instrument of Gaura-Sakti. These times went unnoticed.

Alone on the Jaladuta ship, writing poems and pouring your heart out to Krishna, an effusive flow of transcendental emotion. The shock of a near death experience at sea, heart attacks that you only spoke about a handful of times. You honestly expressed your heart to Krishna – *"I do not know why You have brought me to this terrible place, but clearly You must have a plan. Kindly make me dance as You desire."*

In the early mornings, when the whole world was asleep, you rose, chanted, dictated and penned transcendental truths that would nourish generations to come. But it wasn't just a service for the world – it was an outpouring of transcendental ecstasy. The Srimad-Bhagavatam was your best friend, constant companion and greatest source of happiness. You relished that time alone with Krishna.

In the late evenings, unseen in the public eye and away from the spotlight, you sat in solitude, singing hymns on your harmonium, drowning in the feelings of the illustrious saints of yore. You sang the same line again and again – *"O my Lord I have uselessly wasted my life and thus I have knowingly drunk poison"* – crying for Krishna, a *prema-bhiksu*, beggar of love.

The private life of a pure devotee, ever rooted in a world which is invisible to most people's eyes. In reality, however, you were never alone because your transcendental consciousness meant you traversed this world in the constant company of Sri Krishna and Sri Guru. Your inside and outside were identical. Always with Krishna and effortlessly giving Krishna to others.

We can only give what we have. We can't take the world to a higher place than we've reached internally ourselves. We hold onto you, Srila Prabhupada, and pray you'll introduce us to Krishna. Then we'll try to come back into the world and do something for your glorious mission. Sharing Krishna Consciousness with deep compassion and genuine realisation – emissaries of realised philosophy, touching hearts because our own heart has been touched. Diving deeper and reaching out further. Thank you for gifting us such a beautiful adventure to embark upon.

Eternally indebted, S.B. Keshava Swami

Dear Srila Prabhupada,

Please accept my humble obeisances. All glories to your divine grace!

In my early years as a monk, people would often suggest I leave the monastery and get a 'proper job.' Sometimes it came from the sceptical and cynical, and other times from well-meaning and kind friends. I guess that's what 'normal' people in this world do. For me, however, that path never resonated – to work, earn, save, spend, maintain... and then ultimately lose everything anyway. Of course, there are exemplary spiritualists who use it all for a higher purpose and make a beautiful contribution to the world. I had (and continue to have) incredible respect for them, but personally was looking for something different.

Baffled and confused, I often wondered about the future... what possible alternative could there be? After all, you have to do *something* in life. Thankfully, your divine grace miraculously entered my insignificant existence and flipped it all upside-down. You lent us a different vision, an alternative approach, an engagement to keep us busy and absorbed, morning to night. You gifted us a life of devotional service, the opportunity to engage in selfless sacrifices for the betterment of the world. You showed us how to utilise our abilities and propensities for a higher purpose than just selfish gain. You taught the world that awakening spiritual love can and should be a full-time affair. In Srimad-Bhagavatam you write:

"Once we had the opportunity to meet Visnupada Sri Srimad Bhaktisiddhanta Saraswati Goswami Maharaja and on first sight he requested this humble self to preach his message in the Western countries. There was no preparation for this, but somehow or other he desired it and by his grace we are now engaged in executing his order,

which has given us a transcendental occupation and has saved and liberated us from the occupation of material activities." (SB 3.22.5 Purport)

Srila Prabhupada, you're my boss, the business of Chaitanya-deva has become my occupation and the salary is the gradual awakening of divine love. My colleagues are the saintly, over-time is a pleasure, holidays are unnecessary and the retirement plan is out of this world. May I be more determined and driven than the people out there chasing a million bucks. May I ready myself for more sacrifices than the city sharks who'll 'go to hell and back' to conquer the corporate ladder. May I embrace more risks than those willing to jeopardise everything to realise their greedy ambitions. The words of Srutidharma Prabhu are etched in my heart: *"When the alarm clock goes off, get up, dress up and show up – this is the most important work in the world."*

Bhaktisiddhanta Saraswati Thakur called his triple-staffed sannyasis the *"living mrdangas"* of Sri Chaitanya. He reminded them that their dandas should *"perpetually give forth music at the lotus feet of Sri Guru."* He revealed the inner aspiration to become a *prema-bhiksu,* a beggar of love. Unqualified and unworthy as I am, by your divine grace and the unlimited mercy of your followers, I've been employed in the transcendental occupation. May I honour the opportunity with body, mind and words, holding back nothing and rising to any challenge. Thank you for allowing us to be alive and active in the greatest movement on Earth.

Your small servant, S.B. Keshava Swami

KADAMBA KANANA SWAMI

I recently gave a presentation entitled "four mistakes I made in my life," and entitled the first mistake "helpless means hopeless." I feel as though in the first ten years of my spiritual journey I never really let people into my life. Though I had experienced and empowered spiritual personalities around me, I never took the opportunity to open my heart to their help. Some of it was shyness, perhaps there was also apprehension and, if I'm honest, a good proportion was also pride. I felt my journey was progressing well and there was little need for the input and feedback of others. Later, however, it dawned on me that without the help of more advanced spiritualists, it's practically impossible to reach your full potential. Nobody is self-made.

When I started building a relationship with my spiritual teacher, my guru, I witnessed how new frontiers of the spiritual landscape were opening up for me. He gave vision, inspiration and encouragement... but also correction, challenge and constructive criticism. It wasn't easy, but it was incredibly empowering. I tried to invest in that relationship and the returns were way beyond what I deserve. Here are some of my words of gratitude to my spiritual master, His Holiness Kadamba Kanana Swami (1953-2023).

THE ALL-ROUNDER (FEB 2015)

Dear Maharaja,

Please accept my humble obeisances. All glories to Srila Prabhupada.

You are a dedicated missionary, but also a thoughtful, contemplative and internal renunciate. You can connect with the rich and wealthy life members, and simultaneously inspire the ruffians in city centre. You can give a thought-provoking, penetrating and highly philosophical discourse, and then express the heights of spiritual emotion through your lion-like singing. You are bold and direct, but simultaneously embody deep humility and compassion. You command a deep sense of respect and authority, but always remain very personal, human, friendly and approachable. You are a penetrating and profound thinker, but simultaneously a practical and streetwise manager. You know the art of making spirituality accessible and relevant, while maintaining strict chastity and loyalty to the predecessor teachers.

There is so much to learn from you. Your unique spiritual personality never fails to capture my imagination. I'm not quite sure how, but I have received the inconceivable good fortune of being your formally initiated disciple. I hope I will offer some service in this life to make you smile,

Begging to remain at your transcendental disposal,

Sutapa das

LENDING THE VISION (FEB 2017)

Dear Maharaja

Please accept my humble obeisances. All glories to Srila Prabhupada.

They say we must live life forwards, but we can only understand it when we look backwards. As I reflect upon and remember the beginnings of our relationship, the things you told me, taught me and trained me in, I begin to appreciate my incredible fortune. Canakya Pandita recommends a child be given great love and encouragement in the beginning, then discipline later on, and finally granted independence and friendship. As an expert and loving father, you give us the perfect balance of all these interactions, opening so many doors of opportunity to serve this glorious mission.

You often talk about how the spiritual master expertly delivers a vision for the disciple's life. He can't just run around solving problems and issues, but must craft a bigger and better plan for the pleasure of the Lord. As that plan emerges, the disciple is forced to dig deeper and tap into the spiritual mercy flow to bring it into reality. It's the classic spiritual exchange between guru and disciple, repeated for generations, amongst the most elevated souls in the universe. I am a weak and impoverished soul but connected to your divine self and a line of spotless Vaisnavas. I'm nervous and challenged; I'm not sure how I'll fulfil your desires and make you happy. I'll try to practice strongly, pray deeply and collect blessings wherever I go. After all is said and done, I ultimately rely on you.

Thank you for everything.

"The road to auspiciousness begins with taking shelter of a bona fide spiritual master. In accordance with God's plan, everyone on this earth finds a teacher that meets his or her particular needs and

qualifications... If we are fortunate, if we truly seek out a genuine guru with complete sincerity and persistence, and if we pray feelingly to the Lord to encounter such a spiritual master, then the Lord will surely lead us in this lifetime to a genuine guru, by taking shelter of whom we will be able to attain the greatest blessings." (Srila Bhaktisiddhanta Saraswati Thakur)

I beg to remain, in your transcendental service,

Sutapa das

GIFTS OF THE GURU (FEB 2018)

Dear Maharaja,

Please accept my humble obeisances. All glories to Srila Prabhupada.

"I bow down to the beautiful lotus feet of my spiritual master, by whose causeless mercy I have obtained the supreme holy name, the divine mantra, the service of the son of Sacimata, the association of Srila Svarupa Damodara, Rupa Goswami, and his older brother Sanatana Gosvami, the supreme abode of Mathura, the blissful abode of Vrindavana, the divine Radha-kunda and Govardhana Hill, and the desire within my heart for the loving service of Sri Radhika and Madhava in Vrindavana." (Sri Mukta-caritam, by Srila Raghunatha dasa Gosvami)

Maharaja, in your role as Sri Guru, you have powerfully delivered all the transcendental gifts to us.

Holy Name – some years ago when you started 'Japa Meditations' on your website, you asked me why I wasn't sharing any thoughts there. You then reminded me how I was lacking in my relationship with the holy name and told me – *"you don't have to just chant 16 rounds!"* (Implying that this is just the start, but eventually we should become so attracted that we can't stop chanting). Seeing your example, I get the impetus to invest in my relationship with the holy name.

Chaitanya Mahaprabhu – I once told you that I found it difficult to connect with Gaura-lila. You told me that *"before appreciating Gaura-lila we first have to understand Gaura-tattva!"* Later on, you reassured me: *"if you have a relationship with me, you will definitely have a relationship with Gauranga!"* You opened up the world of Chaitanya Charitamrita for us, embodying the mood and mission of the Golden Avatar.

Goswamis – you often spoke about Srila Prabhupada wanting 25 renunciates just like the Goswamis to reside in and manage the entire Vrindavana project. You took us to Bangladesh, where we connected with our Vaisnava heritage and learnt the glories of Rupa, Sanatana, Narrotama das Thakur and all the other illustrious personalities. You told me why we were making this arduous journey – *"the relationship will go deeper."*

Vrindavana – when you found out that I hadn't visited Vrindavana for many years you called me a *"ghost."* You have always reminded me to connect with the holy places and take shelter of all the divine experiences available there. Through your love for Vrindavana, we also received a glimpse of that abode and now, slowly but surely, we are reawakening our memory that this is our true home.

Krishna – once, just before you were about to give class, I asked you what the theme would be. Your reply: *"Krishna."* You went there and spoke about the markings on Krishna's feet and immersed yourself in the transcendental descriptions of the scriptures. You told me: *"we don't always have to have a theme – sometimes we can just talk about Krishna and bathe in those beautiful narrations."* With your guidance, we are trying to become attached to Krishna.

Thank you for delivering these gifts. I hope I'll have the intelligence, determination and sincerity to take advantage, and offer some service back to you in gratitude.

Begging to remain your servant,

Sutapa das

THE PROOF-READER (JAN 2019)

Dear Maharaja,

Please accept my humble obeisances. All glories to Srila Prabhupada.

Srila Bhaktisiddhanta Saraswati Thakur once said:

"I don't read the book, I read the author. I first check whether the author is authentic. Srila Bhaktivinoda Thakura trained me in proofreading, so I always look for what is right or wrong. But I am not a proof-reader of the press only; I am a proof-reader of the world. I proofread men; I proofread religions. I dissect their faults and try to correct them." (Bhaktisiddhanta Saraswati Thakur)

For me, you are the transcendental proof-reader. Without your interest and intervention, the story of my life would be pretty dull.

Proof-readers cut out the waffle. They edit down long paragraphs into a few short lines. They identify the essence, preserve the substance and throw the rest by the wayside. You do the same in my life. I can talk it up and hype it big, but in front of you, all the superficiality is exposed. Your presence reveals the degree of genuine sincerity, selflessness and sacrifice in my spiritual life. You help me to see where I'm really at.

Proof-readers flag-up errors. They spot typos and grammar issues, fixing the faults to ensure a smooth read. I make mistakes all the time and you skilfully reveal them before they become problematic. You can spot the dangerous attitudes, bad decisions, false assumptions and potential pitfalls. You're one step ahead of the game, clearing the obstacles and ironing out the issues.

Proof-readers bring potency. They help convey the message with maximum impact and clarity. Your years of experience, deep spiritual insight and streetwise eye detects the most efficient, effective and powerful way to move forward in spiritual life. You challenge me to think outside the box, question my modus operandi and bring out the best.

You've given me the plot, I'm trying to write the narrative, but remain ever dependent on you to expertly proofread it. Chop and change as you wish. I hope the story of my life will turn out according to your desire. Thank you for your unlimited encouragement and constant guidance. Without it I'm lost.

I beg to remain, your servant,

Sutapa das

MOVED BY INSPIRATION (MAR 2020)

Dear Maharaja,

Please accept my humble obeisances. All glories to Srila Prabhupada.

We meditate on the spiritual master, who is ever enthused and inspired in Krishna Consciousness.

From my observation, your entire life moves on inspiration. Your reading of scripture is not just informational and analytical, but reflective and profound – continuously mining jewels that touch your heart and speak to you in a very personal way. Your presentation of Krishna Consciousness is not staged and memorised, but fluid and spontaneous – bringing out personal realisations and delivering a genuine discourse based on what moves you. Your kirtans are not just musical and melodious, but a desperate cry for Krishna – an outpouring of spiritual emotion that ushers us into an experience of transcendence. Your guidance is not only based on knowledge and experience, but divinely dictated – through you we receive the messages of Krishna, perfectly illuminating the journey we need to embark on in life. Your unwavering dedication to sharing Krishna Consciousness and helping others is not just a duty or vow but fuelled by genuine care and concern – only an inspired person can embody such compassion by which they transcend material limitations and serve above and beyond what is humanly possible.

Of all our possessions in life, our inspiration and enthusiasm are perhaps the most valuable. You are giving us that in abundance. How inspired you are! We stay close to you and pray that we become inspired as you are, just so we can render some small service to say *"thank you."*

I beg to remain your humble servant,

Sutapa das

THE SPIRITUAL SCULPTOR (MAR 2021)

Dear Maharaja,

Please accept my humble obeisances. All glories to Srila Prabhupada. All glories to you!

Srila Prabhupada said this human form of life is like a block of hardwood and we have to somehow carve Krishna out of it. You are undoubtedly the expert sculptor who has made my life meaningful. Over the years I couldn't ascertain everything you were doing, but looking back I can join all the dots. At every stage you taught, trained and nurtured a spirit within me. You moulded me and overlooked the weaknesses. You carry the mood of Prabhupada and so I'm made of your mercy.

You instructed me to study Bhagavatam and chant with depth, but also highlighted the need to untiringly reach out and be a 'mission-man.' You reminded me to be gentle and kind, but also strong and sharp, ready to take on responsibility and navigate the ISKCON world to make things happen. You told me to stay 'on the ground', close to the masses, but you also stressed the need to preach to devotees, give classes, build teams and take on leadership for greater impact. You pushed me forward and gave me self-confidence but kept me humble by reserving praise for select times. You taught me to work with the devotees and cooperate, but also pressed me to become independently thoughtful and not just 'go with the flow.' What can I say? Absolute spiritual genius.

You've fully equipped me to become an instrument in Prabhupada's mission and now I have to overcome my hesitation and weaknesses. In the beginning you were hands on. In recent years you watch me from afar, but still present as ever, continuing to shape my life beyond the boundaries of time and space. I'm not sure what new surprises you

have lined up, but I know that under your guidance, life becomes one
big adventure in Prabhupada's great mission! Thank you, Maharaja, for giving me life.

Begging to remain, in your service,

Sutapa das

DRAWING OUT DEVOTION (FEB 2022)

Dear Maharaja,

Please accept my humble obeisances. All glories to Srila Prabhupada.

In a recent gathering with teachers, we were discussing what inspires a student to increase their commitment. Quickly, we began drawing on a shining example of this: the beautiful relationship between Bhaktisiddhanta Saraswati Thakur and our Srila Prabhupada.

"Invest in them and offer quality time" one devotee said, reflecting on how Bhaktisiddhanta Saraswati confidentially revealed his heart to Abhay on the banks of Radha Kund. *"Reveal a vision and set a specific goal"* someone else said, drawing on the Thakur's prophetic and pointed command to preach Bhagavata-dharma all over the world. One devotee mentioned *"the leaders own deep level of commitment,"* explaining how Bhaktisiddhanta Saraswati was himself willing to risk his life for missionary conquests and could therefore instill that in others. *"Acknowledgment and encouragement are important"* one preacher said, remembering how Abhay's spiritual master deeply appreciated his disciple's hunger to listen and expertise in writing. How wonderfully Bhaktisiddhanta Saraswati ignited the unrestricted commitment of Srila Prabhupada! Conquered by the spiritual master, he was ready to do anything.

The discussion helped me appreciate how expertly you have inspired commitment within even unwilling souls like me. You've guided, challenged, cared, encouraged, corrected and crafted a bigger vision for our lives then we could have ever conceived of. Your grace has launched us into the electrifying movement of Chaitanya-deva, where the pastimes of the Lord are going on even today.

What can I do to further your vision? How much deeper can I take my commitment? When will I offer you something that will really make you smile? These are the questions on my mind. It may resemble drawing blood from a stone, but thank you for awakening some commitment within this struggling jiva, overlooking my hesitation and resistance. I pray and hope to somehow reciprocate with your tireless efforts and incredible investments. Words fall short, it's time to make a bigger sacrifice. Thank you for believing in me.

Your servant,

Sutapa das

LOVING SERVICE (FEB 2023)

Dear Maharaja,

Please accept my humble obeisances. All glories to Srila Prabhupada.

When I came to Vrindavana for Kartik you made so many arrangements – you sent your driver to the airport, you arranged everything in the room, you personally brought a mat for me to sit on when you saw me chanting on the floor... you even gave a lock to keep the room secure. When you felt the weight of my danda, you gifted me yours which was much lighter... *"the vow is already heavy!"* you said. I was humbled (and uncomfortable) to be on the receiving end of your kind service.

In that trip, living next to you for the six weeks around Kartik, I felt a surge of gratitude. I realised the greatest spiritual master is actually the greatest servant. They give every last bit of energy - physical, emotional, intellectual and spiritual - to lift the disciple higher. We couldn't ask for more... you have given everything and more.

At times you talked about exciting missionary ideas and other times you established serious philosophical truths. One moment would be a heavy instruction and the next a humorous observation of life. Sometimes you interjected and set the record straight, other times you sat back and heard our inputs. Just like Krishna played many roles while instructing Arjuna - sometimes patiently listening, other times sharing 'an opinion,' sometimes coming in as an authoritative instructor, and other times giving independence and choice - you played all the roles. Perfectly. Our relationship with you encompassed all the flavours... but in every situation you were serving us in different ways, empowering us to be alive and involved, active participants in the greatest movement on Earth.

Some months ago you told me *"I'm not leaving you anything in my will... only service."* When I considered whether to return to the UK for the Christmas marathon you told me *"yes, go... we meet in the mission of Mahaprabhu."* Later on you said *"my generation did our bit and had a go... now it's your turn."* You encouraged me to embrace the path of renunciation and said, *"now we're closing all the doors... just so you can open up a whole new world."*

I had no idea where my journey was taking me, but now in hindsight I see a plan all along, masterfully engineered and executed by your divine grace. I'm humbled that you took such a personal interest. I'm amazed by your investment of faith. I'm indebted beyond my capacity to repay. According to Rupa Goswami's science of *bhakti* it all begins with Sri Guru - who gives shelter (*asraya*), initiation (*diksa*) and instruction (*siksa*). The disciple responds by offering service soaked with love (*visrambhena guroh seva*). You did everything for us, now we have to reciprocate with some solid service. As Srila Prabhupada told Visnujana at his initiation ceremony in 1968:

"You are instructed, you are guided, but you have to act. If you don't act there will be no meaning."

Begging to remain absorbed in your transcendental service,

Svayam Bhagavan Keshava Swami

PRESENCE IN ABSENCE (APRIL 2023)

Separation is a mystical concept. In English we have the saying *"out of sight, out of mind."* An alternative adage tells us that ***"absence makes the heart grow fonder."*** It seems that separation can cause some relationships to fade into obscurity, but also ignite other relationships into a burning inferno. The exalted theologians of divine love explain that separation fuels spiritual relationships; a unique ingredient which raises the intensity of connection to its apex. Union and separation are opposite banks on the river of love. Separation intensifies the subsequent union, and in union, the apprehension of separation constantly lurks.

These topics are currently on my mind. I first met Kadamba Kanana Swami over 20 years ago, and on this day, 15 years ago, I formally became his student. He gifted me vision, inspiration and encouragement... but also correction, challenge and constructive criticism. His presence in my life shifted paradigms and opened up new worlds. His physical departure a few weeks ago has naturally left a feeling of vacuum and marks the closing of a chapter. It's hard, but I have to say... the reality of loss is eclipsed by the realisation of how much was received.

In these days, I reflect on how absence can bring about deeper presence. In presence we receive many gifts, but in absence we deepen our appreciation and genuinely utilise those gifts. In presence we are captured by endearing interactions, in absence we're awakened to the beautiful personality and heart behind it all. In presence we establish relationship, in absence we intensify that relationship. The spiritual teacher enters our life and opens many doors. When they disappear, they inspire us to walk through those doors so we can meet them on the other side. The disappearance of the beloved spiritual teacher is an unwelcome gift, inviting and ushering the disciple into an upgraded spiritual connection.

Ironically, this kind of philosophical explanation doesn't pacify the heart. It does, however, stimulate one to explore exciting ways in which deeper presence can be awakened in absence. Relationships of the eternal world deepen, not by amount of time and proximity of space, but by alignment of desire, synergy in service, and genuine love for the Divine.

AUTHOR

Svayam Bhagavan Keshava Swami (S.B. Keshava Swami) is a spiritual author, community mentor, dynamic teacher and worldwide traveller. In 2002, after graduating from UCL (University College London) with a BSc in Information Management, he adopted full-time monastic life to expand his knowledge, deepen his spirituality and share these timeless principles with the wider society.

For over twenty years, Keshava Swami was a resident monk at ISKCON UK's headquarters, Bhaktivedanta Manor. There he pioneered the School of Bhakti, led the monastic training programme and drove forward national outreach projects. He has designed numerous courses on Vedic theology, lifestyle management and spiritual self-development, and has also authored numerous books which bring the ancient wisdom into the modern context.

In 2022, Keshava Swami accepted vows of lifetime renunciation. Nowadays he is a globe-trotter, teaching in universities, corporate firms, government organisations and spiritual communities, bringing wisdom to the places which need it the most. He continues to diligently study the Sanskrit texts, considering how to proliferate spiritual wisdom in a world that is suffocating from materialism.

BOOKS BY S.B. KESHAVA SWAMI

- Gita Life: A Summary of Bhagavad-gita
- IQ, EQ, SQ: Life, the Universe and Everything
- Tattva: See Inside Out
- Tattva2: Old Words Open New Worlds
- Bhakti Life: 18 Simple Steps to Krishna
- Chaitanya-Charitamrita Compact
- Book Bhagavata: The Life Companion
- Gita3: Wisdom that Breathes
- Playground of God
- Loving Life, Embracing Death
- Masterminds of Bhakti (Upcoming)

Books Compiled by S.B. Keshava Swami:

- Veda: Secrets of the East (A.C. Bhaktivedanta Swami Prabhupada)
- In Essence (A.C. Bhaktivedanta Swami Prabhupada)

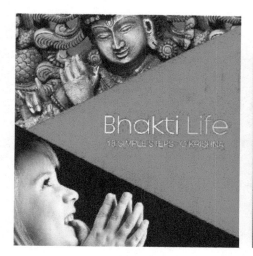

Bhakti Life
18 SIMPLE STEPS TO KRISHNA

EVOLVE YOUR VISION CHANGE YOUR WORLD

IN ESSENCE

CAITANYA CARITĀMRTA
COMPACT

Bhagavad Gita
A Short Summary in Acronyms

Based on Bhagavad Gita as it is by his divine grace
A.C. Bhaktivedanta Swami Prabhupada

Made in the USA
Las Vegas, NV
09 October 2023

78811611R00134